Patterns of Belief

Religions in Society

Eric Carlton

I08941 33

Routledge
Taylor & Francis Group

First published in 1973
by George Allen & Unwin

This edition first published in 2015 by Routledge
2 Park Square, Milton Park, Abingdon, Oxon, OX14 4RN
and by Routledge
711 Third Avenue, New York, NY 10017

Routledge is an imprint of the Taylor & Francis Group, an informa business

Publisher's Note

The publisher has gone to great lengths to ensure the quality of this reprint but points out that some imperfections in the original copies may be apparent.

Disclaimer

The publisher has made every effort to trace copyright holders and welcomes correspondence from those they have been unable to contact.

ISBN 13: 978-1-138-92726-1 (hbk)
ISBN 13: 978-1-138-93432-0 (pbk)

Patterns of Belief 2

Patterns of Belief

Volume 2 Religions in Society

Eric Carlton

London George Allen & Unwin Ltd
Ruskin House Museum Street

First published in 1973

ISBN 0 04 377005 3

Printed in Great Britain
in 11 point Baskerville
by Cox & Wyman Ltd, London, Fakenham and Reading

Contents

Introduction for Teachers *page* 11
Preface 13
1 Is religion 'true'? 17
2 Do people have religious experiences? 33
3 How did religion begin? 49
4 How can religion be analysed? 67
5 What purposes does religion serve? 83
6 How does religion function in different societies? 97
7 Is there such a thing as revelation? 113
References 133
Index 137

Illustrations

1	Baptism	*facing page* 17
2	A Hindu Holy Man	33
3	Haida Indian Totem Pole	49
4	Diana at Ephesus	61
5	The Inquisition	67
6	The Bomb	83
7	Mother and child refugees	93
8	'Telephone book cure' in Kenya	97
9	The Earth seen from the Moon	130

Acknowledgements

The author and publishers are grateful to the following for supplying the photographs numbered below, and for permitting their use. Keystone Press Agency (Plates 1, 2, 7, 8); the Mansell Collection (Plates 3, 4, 5); and the United States Information Service (Plates 6 and 9).

Introduction for Teachers

Sociology is essentially a way of looking at things. It assumes not so much a posture as a stance. It should not—and usually does not—pretend to be a predictive science, but it can claim to provide new perspectives in the study of familiar subjects. This is particularly true in sociological analyses of religion.

Traditional religious ideas involve assumptions which the human sciences can neither validate nor invalidate. Sociology is not concerned with either proving or disproving these assumptions. It does not claim to be able to pronounce upon the possible objective 'truth' of religion. The 'ultimate verities' are quite outside the scope of its enquiries. It is not, therefore, an areligious conspiracy. The sociological approach does not constitute an attempted refutation of religion, but simply a qualification of certain implicit assumptions. It is not out to undermine conventional values, but it does try to take up the position of an impartial enquirer in its examination of those values.

Sociology does maintain that men can infer something of the nature of belief from the nature of *believing*. It insists that religions cannot be meaningfully studied as metaphysical isolates, but only insofar as they find expression in the lives of their adherents. Belief, as such, is notoriously difficult to study. What can be studied are *declarations* of belief, what people say they believe, and the situations in which these declarations are made. For the sociologist, therefore, religion is a social phenomenon. Belief and emotion may give rise to ritual, or perhaps ritual and emotion are intellectualized and codified as belief—this is a difficult and tortuous question.

Whatever, rituals are social acts which can be analysed; religious behaviour is a visible phenomenon which, unlike belief, is susceptible to certain kinds of analysis.

The orientations of this book are intended merely to complement those of a more traditional kind. It is concerned with the ideologies of religious systems, and it is also concerned with the ways in which these ideologies may be conditioned by identifiable psycho-social factors. Systems are structured by particular determinants, and function in examinable ways. It is the empirical manifestations of ideology which must be the main foci of sociological enquiry. This is not to argue that there are no superempirical elements in religion. It is simply that these elements cannot be shown to derive from identifiable sources, and therefore their demonstration and interpretation must continue to remain frustratingly ambiguous. It is the task of this book to show something of the nature of this problem, and both the extent and the limits of its illumination, by a comparative socio-historical approach.

This is hardly, therefore, a Religious Education text in the conventional sense. But it could be used by specialist and non-specialist alike either in Religious Education or General Studies. It is not written to cover any known syllabus, and to this extent it may be somewhat anticipatory. But it could prove to be a useful introductory text for sixth forms, and for Further Education and College of Education students. The nature of its appeal must be ultimately determined by its value as an aid to already established courses, and its capacity to elucidate some of the perennial and perplexing problems of a secular but still curious society.

Preface

It was Aristotle, the Greek philosopher and scientist, who long ago suggested that the best judge of a meal was not the cook who had prepared it, but the guests who had to eat it. He meant by this that ordinary people are the best judges of those things which directly affect them. The experts may have their say, but ultimately all such matters—and he particularly had political issues in mind—must stand or fall on the basis of their relevance and their utility.

Religion is one of those subjects upon which everyone has opinions. There are some things we leave to the experts, particularly scientific matters in which we can claim no special competence. But religion does not come into this category. Questions of practice and belief *have* to be considered by everyone, however perfunctorily, at some time or another. Such considerations may be hasty and superficial, but everyone faces them if only to dismiss them.

What applies to people also applies to various academic disciplines. Some of these, mainly the natural or physical sciences, will have little or nothing to say about religion. They do make indirect allusions and sometimes even direct statements where their findings appear either to support or to conflict with certain religious assumptions. But, in general, they avoid issues which are outside their frames of reference. The social sciences, on the other hand, often have quite a lot to say on the subject. But they too have their own special orientations and their own limited spheres of competence.

Religion is a ubiquitous phenomenon, it has existed everywhere at all times, and cannot therefore be ignored by students of human behaviour. The particular contribution of the social sciences in this respect has been in their method of approach to the subject. As sciences, they are essentially *inferential*, that is to say they do not assume the existence of god or the gods, but infer their existence as objects of worship and belief from the practices and statements of people. In other words, the social sciences are only really concerned with behaviour which can be studied, and data which can be empirically validated. They are not really interested in theological speculation except insofar as it is believed to affect human action.

This summarizes the orientation of this book. Whatever may be the 'truth' of religion in some objective sense, it is an inescapable social fact. As such, it can be examined historically and comparatively, and—above all—scientifically, for a science is to be judged by its method rather than its capacity for prediction. This is not, therefore, a study of the things people believe, which is what is usually conceived as religion, but an examination of the circumstances in which these beliefs arise and the ways in which they are maintained and perpetuated. Such a study may or may not give us insights into the possibility or otherwise of the supernatural, but it should make us more aware of the ambiguities of the human condition.

Chapter One

Is religion 'true'?

Perhaps one of the tragedies of life is that we have the intelligence to frame certain apparently simple questions like the child's, 'What is God like?', which cannot be satisfactorily answered even after a lifetime of study. The question 'Is religion "true"?' falls into this category. Indeed, there is a kind of mathematical complexity involved in the asking and answering of this kind of question. Sometimes a multitude of problems gives rise to a single question which then becomes the focus of a certain kind of concentrated attention. The question itself, in turn, generates a whole range of possible answers and yet further questions.

The purpose of this book is to examine this kind of problem from a particular point of view. The aim here is to consider the implications of the social reality of religion. But before we do so, we must give a little time to the fundamental problem of what we mean by 'truth'.

At a secondary level, the problem can be regarded as a purely semantic one, that is to say, it is really concerned with the meaning of words. But at a primary level, there is rather more to it than this. We know that there are different kinds of 'truth' (see Volume 1, particularly Chapter Two), but an examination of these cannot avoid the basic assumption behind the question, namely, that 'out there' there may be some kind of supramundane reality which humans only dimly perceive.

In this chapter, then, we are going to look at the problem in this 'reverse' order by first of all considering some of the different possible interpretations of the idea of 'truth'.

SUBJECTIVE TRUTH

The notion of subjective truth is really quite a simple one. Take, for example, the question 'Is Labour policy true?' This initially demands some clarification as to exactly what Labour policy is at specific times on specific issues. Like Tory policy—or any other policy for that matter—there is a tendency for this to change as the occasion demands. You may then argue that there is surely something unchanging which underlies Labour policy—something fundamental which is more distinctively 'Labour'. In this case, it would probably be better to rephrase the original question. Thus it might become more meaningful as 'Is Socialist philosophy true?' This suggests that there is a basic orientation in Socialist thinking which is identifiable and which is significantly different from other philosophies.

Let's consider the implications of this idea one at a time, and see how they relate to this whole notion of 'truth'. Firstly, to be able to distinguish a difference—even a significant difference—in any mode of thinking, political or otherwise, does not necessarily mean that it is 'true'. This point is obvious. Secondly, and a little less obviously, even political philosophies can be very flexible when it comes to meeting the demands of actual political situations. The Party line will be modified; idealists—and even politicians may be idealists—can be practical men. Even a superficial reading of the history and development of political movements will show how this has operated. In effect, the philosophy, the 'truth', is usually adapted and rationalized in the interests of practical necessity. Thirdly, and this is the point that particularly concerns us here, to speak of the truth *in* Socialist philosophy should not lead us to the conclusion that Socialist philosophy is always and forever 'true'. It certainly cannot be guaranteed to 'work' in all circumstances. We will return to this theme in Chapter Six, but it will suffice here to state that the notion of an *objective* truth in any political philosophy is quite without foundation. It cannot really be sustained as an argument. To say 'Socialist philosophy is true' really means Socialist philosophy is true for you, it is your solution for society's ills. In fact, other solutions might work equally well, if they gained general support. It was George Bernard Shaw who once insisted that he could think of several schemes over tea for putting the world right, the difficulty was getting other people to agree with them.

It should be clear from the foregoing argument that questions of value are not subject to experimental proof. Ultimately, we think a thing is 'good' or 'right' for reasons that are not easily testable. A philosophy or a policy may be seen to 'work' in particular circumstances, but this does not and cannot validate its truth beyond or outside the context in which it has been operated. For example, the qualified success of Fascism in Italy in the thirties in 'making the trains run on time' was certainly no guarantee that it would work equally well elsewhere.

Similarly, in the arts, the impression of what is 'good' must remain largely a matter of opinion. The beauty or artistic merit of a painting or piece of music cannot be assessed in scientific terms. They remain 'in the eye of the beholder'—such values are held to be subjective. This argument is also applicable to questions of morality. The problems here are much more complicated, but basically we observe certain moral values because we think we should. Morality is essentially a very subjective business. Of course in this area, there are all sorts of pressures brought to bear by society to ensure that there is a basic conformity on certain issues. This is not only a matter of conviction, it is also a matter of convenience. But it still holds that such values as honesty and fairness cannot be *shown* to be 'right' in any scientific sense, even if they do 'work' in most situations.

All this is not to say that there are no standards in politics, in art or morality or whatever. What is being maintained here is that if there are such standards, their 'truth' or otherwise cannot be demonstrated in ways that will satisfy every enquirer. But then there may well be 'truths' other than 'scientific' truths.

SCIENTIFIC TRUTH

It has been argued [1] that for a proposition to be considered as scientific it must necessarily also be 'falsifiable'. That falsifiability should be the main criterion for all scientific statements means that all such statements must be susceptible of falsification as the result of new discoveries or further experimentation. Statements which are not open to falsification in this way are *ipso facto* non-scientific. For instance, advertising claims—especially those of a highly generalized nature—are rarely capable of falsification. Until recently in the Midlands, it was not uncommon to see such an advertisement which proclaimed the legend that 'M——— Sausages are the Finest in the World'. One can imagine representatives of M——— fanning out all over the globe intent on establishing unfavourable comparisons with their sausages. A gastronomic feat never to be equalled. It hardly needs labouring that for various reasons, such a claim is hardly capable of verification.

Similarly, if an eccentric space-watcher claims to have had messages from an extra-terrestrial source, or a tragic Joan of Arc insists that she must obey her 'voices', the 'truth' or otherwise of these statements must be regarded as *non*-scientific simply because they are not open to empirical verification. The facts are just not available to disprove them. The notion of falsification does not mean, of course, that a statement or proposition will be disproved, only that such a possibility must exist. In the non-scientific statements we have considered neither verification nor refutation exist even as a possibility—at least not by any known experimental method.

There is, however, a logical error that one could make in all this. In our time, there is a very strong tendency to equate that which is scientifically verifiable with 'truth'. This can be a mistake for two reasons. Firstly, even scientific truth changes (as noted in Vol. 1) as experimental methods become increasingly sophisticated and new discoveries are made. We know that some 'scientific statements' have been shown to be untrue—or at least inaccurate and therefore unmeaningful. These would include such one-time verities as 'nature abhors a vacuum', 'biological species are immutable', 'atoms are indivisible and indestructible', and so on [2]. The second reason is that it is a logical fallacy to assume that non-scientific necessarily means untrue. One of the main purposes of this discussion is to try to establish that there are 'truths' other than those which can be verified by science. We surely all know this from experience. For example, countless people this week alone will say to someone, 'I love you', and there is no way of verifying the 'truth' or otherwise of that statement. All the so-called evidences for 'genuine' love can be attributed to other emotions or motives. Self-sacrifice, insistent attention, deep concern, the need for physical contact, all these may derive from alternative 'causes'. The desire for sexual intercourse, for all its importance, is probably the least likely evidential candidate, seeing as it is everywhere present for a variety of reasons which may have nothing to do with 'love' as it is traditionally conceived. Yet despite all this, are we to say that love—because it cannot be experimentally verified—does not exist?

Science deals with facts and things, those entities and materials which are susceptible to quantification and measurement by its own changing and pre-determined methods. The verification principle which underlies all scientific method is not able to validate aesthetic or artistic values, neither is it capable of evaluating moral or spiritual values. This may be attempted by recourse to a process of 'reductionism', that is the attempt to reduce moral and spiritual values to non-moral and non-spiritual terms. Thus 'good' may be explained naturalistically as that which meets with social approval or that which brings the greatest happiness to the greatest number, and so on. In other words, 'good' has no value in itself, but is to be regarded as the product of certain human attitudes or assumed desires. Similarly, spiritual values may be reduced to equally vague psychological notions such as 'wish-fulfilment' [3], but with little success. It's like trying to reduce a Rembrandt painting to the pigments and the canvas; very few would dispute that such works of art are more than the material or physical constituents which comprise them. Likewise, there are values and experiences which are not, by their very nature, capable of being neatly codified or quantified. This shows no lack on the part of science, it is not to be blamed for this inadequacy, but its methods are just not designed to cope with non-empirical phenomena. It can establish its own truths—truths which are of considerable consequence for human society—but there are other kinds of truth, as we all know. It would be a very rash person who maintained that science, in its present developing form, 'knows' all that is worth knowing.

DIDACTIC TRUTH

This literally means 'teaching truth'. Didactic truth particularly applies to truths contained in parables, allegories and certain kinds of myth. For instance, younger children reading the Book of Genesis sometimes ask, 'Is the Adam and Eve story true?' The apparently contradictory answer is 'Yes—and no'. That is to say, although the story is not historically true, it *teaches* important truths. Few would any longer argue for the historicity of an actual Adam and an actual Eve. Any intelligent reading of the text shows that they are symbolic characters as are also the 'serpent' and the 'tree of the knowledge of good and evil'. The Garden of Eden myth is really an Everyman story, indeed the word Adam means 'the man'. Among other things, it teaches that choice and decision-making are crucial acts which can lead to catastrophic consequences. The capacity for choice must involve the capacity to make the wrong decision. Interpreted in this way, it has modern, existential implications; it suggests that men mature or 'become' as they make daily decisions which affect their own lives and the societies of which they are members.

A similar view may be taken of parables, sometimes called fables (as in the stories of Aesop), and allegories. In allegories, there is an obvious symbolism, where people, places and things represent something else, for instance, in the allegory of the

Sower (wrongly termed a parable, Mark 4), or in John Bunyan's *Pilgrim's Progress*. Parables, on the other hand, may be a little more difficult. The story, as such, may or may not be historically true. In a sense, it doesn't really matter. The point of the parable is the central truth or lesson it contains; the details of the story may actually be irrelevant. The 'moral' may not always be that easy to discern; this is particularly the case in New Testament parables. For example, the point of the parable of the Labourers in the Vineyard (Matthew 19) is certainly not immediately evident. Or again, the parable of the Prodigal Son (Luke 15) has been consistently misinterpreted. Indeed, it is a common error to suppose that Jesus usually taught in parables so that people would understand him better. The evidence sometimes even suggests the reverse (Mark 4: 10–13).

Truth, therefore, in this didactic or teaching sense, may be seen in terms of insights and perceptions. The medium of the message, which can be a poem or symbolic myth or whatever, may be simply a vehicle whereby the central truth is transmitted. This is a simple but important point to grasp, because it is particularly relevant to religions whose rituals and scriptures tend to make use of the indirect, representational approach.

This is certainly the case in Christianity where church art and architecture combine to enhance the worshipper's sense of awe and awareness. The use of 'elements' such as water, bread and wine in symbolic rituals reinforce this sense of 'otherness' and, in their own ways, convey the 'message' for those who have been initiated into their meanings.

Even in extreme Nonconformist churches where these psycho-spiritual aids are largely absent and where the architecture and the decor are plain and the worship is simple, particular 'truths' are still being communicated. Nonconformist churches and sect meeting-centres tend to be less ornate and the worship forms more austere than others. They stress the 'directness' and simplicity of communion with God. The emphasis is not so much on the sacraments as on the 'word' which is preached; this is seen as a more effective medium for the transmission of the 'truth'. Nonconformity tends to inculcate a kind of puritanism which seeks to divest worship of much of its 'mystique', and concentrates instead on instruction of a more conventional kind. But the symbolism is still present in the language of the hymns and prayers, and the evangelical emphasis on spiritual-emotional experience has its own rather intangible meanings for the believer. 'Truth' can obviously be conveyed in many ways.

UTILITARIAN TRUTH

Utilitarian 'truths' are really truths of convenience. They are the truths which we contrive and accept for the smooth and orderly running of everyday affairs.

Take, for instance, simple concepts of measurement. We all know that there is no actual inch or foot or yard, no actual pound, stone or hundredweight. Indeed, we are only too well aware in decimalization controversies that other societies use other standards of measurement with comparative satisfaction. We employ the standards we do for sheer convenience, and we can—and perhaps will—abandon them if others are shown to be more convenient. Concepts such as these, therefore, are neither true nor false, they are merely more or less useful. And in being useful, and therefore accepted, they can be regarded as 'true' for practical purposes. Insofar as they have a kind of utility in society, they are consequently true for us.

A very similar view may be taken of certain common social practices which have become venerated by time and tradition, and are therefore regarded as 'true' for our society. Let's take two such practices which are quite diverse in kind, but which share certain common features in that both have been sanctified by religion, and both have been accepted almost without question in our own society until relatively modern times, namely, christening and the institution of the monarchy.

Christening, or infant baptism, seems to have had its origins in the days of the Roman persecution of the early Christians. In primitive Christianity, adult baptism as a sign or witness of repentance and conversion to the new faith seems to have been the norm. But later, during periods of proscription, parents understandably wanted the rite for their children as well. They were perilous times, and the children might never see adulthood, so the normal practice was waived in favour of natural sentiment. The earlier belief in personal conversion seems to have been modified in accordance with the changes in practice, so that children could now be 'christened'—in a potential or qualified form—on the strength of their parents' faith and confession.

The practice has continued in much the same form ever since, even though it has no direct New Testament basis. Nowadays, it is very much a social convention, and it is not at all uncommon for even avowed agnostics to have their children christened as a matter of form. It's almost as though they were taking out a kind of celestial insurance against the possibility of it all being true after all! Regarded in this way, to have the baby sprinkled doesn't do any harm, and it might even do a lot of good.

Probably very few people now believe that it is possible to 'Christianize' a child in this way, if indeed they accept the Christian ideas implicit in the symbolism itself. To very many people, it is a way of 'giving the child a name', although in fact this is done when the child is registered with the appropriate authority. There are still lingering superstitions associated with this act which is now little more than a matter of convenience. It expresses a *social* 'truth' about the nature of the family and ways in which it is organized and integrated in our society. To a lesser extent, it may represent an act of thanksgiving for another—and perhaps unwanted—addition. It can and should represent the genuine intention of the parents to dedicate themselves conscientiously to the task of parenthood. How well it is actually understood in these terms, is probably impossible to determine.

The institution of the monarchy comes into much the same category. It is notoriously difficult to advance a logical case for such an institution. There are good enough theories as to how it *originated*, and a case can be made for its retention on grounds of practicality, but reasoned arguments for its rightful place in modern society are singularly lacking. The fact that royalty and all its traditional—and perhaps unnecessary—appendages are retained probably owes much more to a subtle amalgam of sentiment and convenience than anything else.

Historically, this institution was buttressed and justified in religious terms. But although we have come a long way from the seventeenth-century doctrine of the Divine Right of Kings, the extent to which the mystique is still present can be seen in the coronation ceremony. No one knows just how many people really believe that God has set particular rulers over us. It is indeed hard to reconcile God's omniscience with his good intentions when one considers the motley lot with which England alone has been blessed over the last thousand years.

Again, the question of utility is involved. Monarchs no longer rule, their right to govern is severely restricted and even their public pronouncements—where possible—are carefully vetted. Despite their enormous private wealth, they are, in a very real sense, public servants. Their task, in effect, is to act as titled public relations people, and symbolize, in Britain at least, the mythical unity of the English-speaking nations in a barely existent commonwealth. The institution of the monarchy has, therefore, a kind of pragmatic truth, that is to say, it can be seen to be something which works—admittedly in a rather qualified way—in given situations. To the extent, therefore, that it has social relevance, it constitutes a form of social truth.

To return, then, to the original problem of the 'truth' or otherwise of religion. We can now see that religion can be true and/or untrue in various ways. It is claimed by believers in religious systems that religion has 'spiritual' truth. Their argument is that religion—or the particular religion to which they personally subscribe—has an objective validity which cannot be assessed in scientific terms. The basic assumption of this argument is that if God could be explained, God wouldn't be God. This position is summed up very well in the insistence of Jesus that 'God is Spirit and they that worship him must worship in spirit and truth' (John 4: 24). In other words, the 'truth' of the spiritual is not susceptible to empirical tests, and cannot be judged by non-spiritual standards.

This approach may be a sound one—it is certainly rather humbling—but it does present two main difficulties. The first is that people still continue to seek experimental proofs, and the second—which has led to untold confusion—is that religious people have sometimes tried to provide such proofs. These proofs can be categorized as:

(i) Cosmological proofs
(ii) Biblical proofs
(iii) Historical proofs
(iv) Phenomenological proofs
(v) Experimental proofs.

These are high-sounding technical terms which can be explained without too much difficulty. It is worth pursuing these points which raise several important issues, especially for Christianity, so we will consider them briefly under these headings.

(i) *Cosmological Proofs.* These concern problems about the origins and nature of the universe, and the meaning of existence. These fundamental questions are largely unanswerable in our present state of knowledge, although they are questions which men are bound to go on asking. It cannot be established that God must exist because the universe does, even less can the nature of the universe—whatever that is—tell us anything about the nature of the deity. After all, to human experience, the universe has strange contradictory features—it appears as both good and evil, though as that great scientist, Albert Einstein, once observed, 'God may be subtle, but he is never malicious'.

Such questions may not admit of any meaningful answers at the present time, but they do pose one interesting problem which should concern us, namely that we have no other alternative but to accept the idea of either an eternal Creation or an eternal Creator (note that the term 'eternal' is used because it logically disposes of the tedious question 'Who made God?'). All other theories are really variations on these two. Of course, in our scientific age, there is a strong tendency to accept the eternal Creation view and repudiate the notion of an eternal Creator which poses some very awkward questions. After all, we can see the Creation, but the Creator remains something of a mystery. But this does not help us much with the problem of origins. If we accept the theory of an eternal Creation, we are immediately confronted with some further awkward questions, namely:

(a) Even if we start with just one atom, can we even begin to explain its origins? Does an eternal atom make sense?
(b) How can we account for forces which caused it to change and develop?
(c) How can we explain what determined the direction of that development?
(d) How has it come about that our single hypothetical atom came to 'contain' its universe-forming potential?
(e) Can intelligence derive from non-intelligence?

(ii) *Biblical Proofs*. These really speak for themselves. People who argue in favour of any of the 'higher religions' often resort to their scriptures for support. The Bible particularly is still regarded by many as inspired literature, and by a minority as a foundation for faith and morals which is not to be questioned. This view, of course, is hardly satisfactory for those who want experimental proofs.

The notion of Biblical or scriptural proof is closely allied to that of:

(iii) *Historical Proofs*. For those who advance them these take two forms. The first involves the implicit assumption of the historicity of the Biblical or scriptural records. This is a very difficult and extremely complex subject which is still being debated. The accuracy of historical details, is still in question, but, in general, it is not the historical record which is primarily in dispute, but the ways in which this is to be interpreted. The second takes the form of an argument for 'the hand of God in history'. Its advocates maintain that God's activity can be seen in certain historical events, although exactly which ones depends very much on who is doing the advocating. The events may be Biblical, for example the Crossing of the Red Sea, or non-Biblical, like the successful retreat of the British Expeditionary Force at Dunkirk in 1940. Yet again, the *basic* historical facts are not the main points of debate, but the interpretation of those facts or purported facts. As proofs of religion they must remain inadequate.

(iv) *Phenomenological Proofs.* These are, to some extent, related to both Biblical and historical proofs. Those who adopt this kind of argument, insist that various known and well-attested phenomena point to the truth of religion. These would include for example, such things as 'speaking in tongues'—which will be dealt with later—and believed communications with the 'other side' practised mainly by Spiritualists. These are held to be incontestable proofs by those who accept them.

(v) *Experiential Proofs.* These are not really proofs at all, as such, but really subjective arguments which maintain that there are certain truths which some people sense within, and which are not open to verification or otherwise in experimental terms. They raise the difficult question of the extent to which intuitive experience is a kind of knowledge.

We can summarize all these arguments by saying that there are no indisputable proofs, otherwise there would certainly be more believers than there are. All proofs are contestable, although some proofs do provide interesting bases for the possibility of religious 'truth'. The fact of the matter is that there are no demonstrable proofs of religion except for those people who are predisposed to accept them. A particular 'miracle', for example, may be acceptable to those who are prepared, in advance, to believe in the possibility of 'miracles'.

To those who are not, such an event will be rationalized in naturalistic ways; it will be 'explained' non-religiously.

In this book, the intention is not to view religion spiritually, but to look at it in social terms; the following discussion will therefore be conducted along sociological lines.

The sociologist is not able to pronounce on the spiritual truth or otherwise of religion, for this concerns the 'ultimate verities' which are outside the purview of sociology. Instead, he is concerned with the social forms and implications of religious beliefs. In his own personal life, he may or may not hold religious beliefs, but as a student of society he must try to maintain some degree of impartiality and 'see' religion objectively. Needless to say, this is a notoriously difficult exercise for a number of reasons, not least of all because as an observer it is almost impossible for him to disassociate himself from the society of which he is a part. Nevertheless, the sociologist—whatever his personal views—recognizes the *social validity* of religion. It is something people live by and die for. It may or may not be objectively true; the gods may or may not exist. There may be nothing actually 'out there', but religious beliefs and practices are social facts, and must therefore be of some concern to those who wish to understand human society. Churches, mosques, synagogues and temples exist, people everywhere persist with worship. An incalculable variety of rituals are performed—why? These facts demand at least an attempted explanation. Whatever the other 'truths' of religion might be, its very presence constitutes a social truth which can hardly be denied.

It is for this reason, that sociology tends to concentrate its attention on practices rather than beliefs, on patterns of behaviour rather than statements of faith. It is not that beliefs are unimportant, it is merely that pronouncements of this kind are incapable of verification; they have no reference outside themselves. For instance, if a man says, 'I believe in God' or 'I believe in life after death', it really tells us very little about him. These beliefs may or may not produce particular kinds of behaviour. In the Christian tradition, this could mean that certain beliefs of the adherent will give rise to particular practices such as praying and going to church, but unbelievers also sometimes pray and go to church, and believers sometimes don't do either. In fact, it is very difficult to connect *causally* any belief with a particular practice, even though there may be a psychologically plausible association between them. This is not to say that the connection is a false one, merely that it is difficult to prove.

It has already been emphasized that concerning the possible objective truth of religion, there can be no experimental certainty. Sociology, therefore, tends to ignore theological questions of the 'What is God like?' and 'What is the nature of the after-life?' type, and confines itself to what it regards as more meaningful issues such as, 'How do believers organize themselves?' and 'What is the relationship between these organizations and the general structure of society?'

Sociology is concerned, therefore, with problems which can be investigated, and with questions which will yield some kind of answer. It does not limit itself to the study of any one kind of religious system, but regards them comparatively. At the same time, it views each system within the context of the society in which it has developed, and tries to give due weight to other factors, economic, political and so on, which must impinge on religious beliefs and practices. In short, religion can not only be seen as history or myth, but also in terms of its social functions. Consequently, sociology studies the behavioural expressions of religion and the possible determinants of its many forms. But in all this, however, it should be stressed that in arriving at its—often tentative—conclusions, it has only studied religion in its social expression. Anything beyond this is a matter of personal conviction, and that is something beyond the scope of any scientific discipline.

2 A Hindu Holy Man

Chapter Two

Do people have religious experiences?

It can be argued that all religious beliefs and practices derive from the religious experience. The actual experiences differ with the individuals and societies in question, but very generally speaking they do share certain common features. On the other hand, the explanations given to account for the experiences differ enormously, and so, of course, do the beliefs and practices which follow. In this, and to some extent the following chapter, we are going to look at various kinds of purported religious experience, and try to get a clearer idea of the problems associated with them.

For simplicity of analysis, we can classify religious experiences as:

(i) Mystical or solitary experiences
(ii) Group-generated experiences
(iii) Artificially induced experiences—including drug-induced experiences.

Mystical or Solitary experiences

These are rarely entirely solitary. The person who makes such a claim may insist that the experience has occurred in isolation, but usually that person is to be found within some kind of religious tradition. The experience itself may be a solitary experience but the individual in question is normally someone who—in general terms—subscribes to the beliefs, if not the practices, of a known religious tradition. And furthermore, that tradition—or at least some people within it—will be willing to accept the possibility of that individual's experience, because such phenomena are *expected* within the tradition.

Take, for example, the experiences and purported miracles associated with the shrine at Lourdes. The greatest care is taken by the Roman Catholic authorities to authenticate the miracles which it is claimed have taken place at Lourdes, with the result that relatively few of these phenomena are pronounced genuine. Any other kinds of mystical experiences which accompany visits to the shrine must be regarded as barely anticipated by-products and may not need authenticating unless the private experience threatens to become—for some reason—public property.

Within Roman Catholicism, mysticism and mystical experiences may actually be encouraged providing both the form and the consequences of these experiences are in line with the tradition of the Church. It is indeed a mark of esteem to be 'given' visions, and it may even be thought that the recipient has been blessed with a special 'capacity' for such experiences. However, those which deviate from the norm may be condemned as heresy or, at best, be regarded with tolerant amusement—depending on circumstances. Joan of Arc, for example—a rather militant mystic—would almost certainly have fared better in our own time. She hardly deserved the stake for obeying her 'voices', but at least this ensured her reputation for posterity. Today, she might have got as far as spearheading a student protest, although its much more likely that she would have ended up in some provincial out-patients' department.

'Experiences' must both conform to and support the tradition. The mystic is permitted to have visions of the appropriate saints or even the Virgin Mary, but 'messages' from renegade Protestant reformers have not been much in evidence with Catholics. The interesting thing is that the socio-psychological patterns of expectation are such that not only are the 'right' kind of phenomena expected, they are also usually *experienced.*

Of course, this is true of traditions other than Catholicism. In fact, it is a phenomenon which is found in all kinds of religious systems in both complex and simple societies. For instance, the tradition among some nomadic peoples in north-eastern Asia is that their 'shamans' or holy men are capable of working themselves into a state of frenzy. Not infrequently they are epileptics. Thus aspiring shamans tend to develop the characteristics which are expected of them. Their influence with the gods, and consequently their reputations with the tribes depend upon their capacity for ecstasies—of the right kind.

Mystical experiences, therefore, although essentially personal phenomena, usually derive from and conform to the expectations of a known religious tradition.

We are here concerned primarily with the ways in which purported religious experiences occur and the nature of their behavioural expressions. We cannot pronounce on the 'truth' or otherwise of these experiences, we can only observe their *social* consequences. (See also Chapter Seven.) In very general terms, mystical experiences serve either to: (i) reinforce the faith of the recipient and/or (ii) inspire the recipient to share this faith with others in specific ways.

The case of (i) is fairly straightforward. The result of the particular experience will be the strengthening of an inner faith which, as far as can be assessed, will have purely personal consequences. For instance, Paul writes (in 2 Corinthians 12: 2–5) 'I know a man in Christ who, fourteen years ago, had the experience of being caught up into the Third Heaven. I don't know whether it was an actual physical experience, only God knows that. All I know is that this man was caught up into paradise . . . this man heard words that cannot, and indeed must not, be translated into human speech. I am honestly proud of an experience like that, but I have made up my mind not to boast of anything personal . . .' It is a reasonable assumption from that context, that the man in question was the apostle himself. The entire business is all very strange, and is made even more mysterious by the curious language ('Third Heaven' etc.) and by the writer's insistence, after having whetted everybody's appetites, that he is not going to say anything more about it. It is a personal matter, he insists, and humility dictates that it must stay that way.

For our purposes, the possible situations suggested by (ii)

are far more important because the social consequences of the experience are more significant. Some well-known historical 'types' come within this category:

(a) *The Guru:* is a type of spiritual teacher or holy man to be found mainly in Hinduism and Sikhism, who may lay claim to specific spiritual experiences. As in any faith—and Hinduism especially could be regarded as a collection or composite of many faiths—there are different kinds of spiritual teachers. Very generally, gurus are of two kinds: those who are only marginally linked with the recognized faith and those who quite definitely come within a specific tradition.

The guru usually gathers around him a small band of followers who may or may not be loosely organized along democratic lines. Primarily, however, the loyalty of the disciples is to the master himself, and the basis of this loyalty is the guru's own spiritual experience and his ability as a teacher. The distinctive nature of his 'message' is important. His personality and his example hold the group together. If he dies or his personal qualities—sometimes termed 'charisma'—appear to fade, there is a strong possibility that the band will disintegrate. If, on the other hand, the guru is particularly successful, a new movement or a new faith will have been born. In the fifteenth century, for example, a guru named Vallabha founded a Hindu sect, the Vallabhis, which cultivated the worship of god as Krishna, the lover of pleasure. They threw off many of the restraints of some other forms of Hinduism, and maintained that the body should be indulged and engaged in erotic pleasures. Indeed, the rules governing the behaviour of the gurus of the movement were particularly advantageous—for the gurus. Followers deemed it an honour to be allowed to present the leader with their virgin daughters or newly married wives for sexual purposes. The pendulum had taken a full swing away from the asceticism of many other Hindu sects to the full sensual expression of the new movement.

(b) *The Prophet:* has many features in common with the

guru. Usually he will have links with a traditional faith, even if in some instances these links are rather tenuous. Prophets, however, tend to emerge during periods of national crisis or spiritual declension. Their mission is often seen as something quite specific, and when this is completed they may return to their original way of life. The eighth-century Hebrew prophet, Amos, who was a sheep-breeder and small farmer in the southern kingdom of Judah, left his work to prophesy in the prosperous northern kingdom of Israel. He criticized the self-satisfied affluence of the aristocracy, and saw the growing menace of the Assyrian power in the Middle East as God's warning to a people suffering from moral decay. The danger materialized some forty years or so after the prophecy when Israel was invaded and many of her people were either killed or deported. But long before this, the prophet, having said what he felt had to be said, had returned to his flocks and vines in his native Tekoa in the South. Judah's turn was to come later.

It is a common error to suppose that the prophet is someone who foretells the future in some general sense. More commonly, he is someone who speaks out on specific issues in particular situations. The evil, as he sees it, may either be present or regarded as an imminent danger to be faced. His utterances, though full of forebodings, often contain a note of hope. This is certainly the case with Hebrew prophecy which unfailingly reminds the hearers that they can be spared the 'wrath to come' if only they will repent and turn from their evil ways.

In more recent times, prophets have arisen in certain predictable situations. For example, in the USA, the teacher of the 'Great Message to the Iroquois', a prophet called Handsome Lake, emerged with a plea for peace whilst other Indian prophets were urging the tribes to destroy the Europeans and restore Indian supremacy [1].

The social functions of prophets, therefore, can be seen as primarily that of reform and the task of helping the group (or nation or race) in their adjustment to a new and difficult situation. In all this, the prophet may act alone or with a group of followers whom he has impressed with his teaching. As in the case of the guru, the movement, such as it is, will hinge on the charisma of the leader which itself centres on his conviction of personal 'revelation'. It is *his* mystical experience which holds the movement together.

(c) *The Messiah:* is 'related' to the prophet, but they can be differentiated on one particular issue. For whereas the prophet may claim that his message is from God or the gods, the Messiah either claims to *be* divine, or else this claim is made for him by his followers. The word messiah is Hebrew and really connotes an anointed or appointed saviour or deliverer; the Greek term Christos means virtually the same thing.

Messiahs tend to appear in much the same situations as prophets, and their social functions are therefore very similar. Although they too will be linked with an accepted religious tradition, their messages usually have a wider appeal than those of a prophet, and they are often distinctive enough to justify the formation of a separate movement. The mission of a prophet, as we have noted, can be very specific and therefore rather transient, whereas that of the messiah will probably have a more lasting effect. Prophets come and go, and sometimes revert to their former occupations—after all, they regard themselves only as men. By definition, messiahs are something more than men, so it's usually a case of once a messiah always a messiah.

The claims made by most would-be messiahs have attracted very little attention. One estimate [2] suggests that from the first to the twentieth centuries, there have been as many as forty-nine messiahs in the Jewish tradition alone. This compares with another estimated forty-nine among the much more numerous Muslims and forty-six in the Christian tradition. On the other hand, a few of these men have made an ineradicable impression on world affairs, not least of all Jesus of Nazareth who, interestingly enough, emerged during a period in which there was a positive surfeit of self-proclaimed messiahs. Why these are now long-forgotten non-entities by comparison with this obscure carpenter whose life and teachings have radically influenced the course of history, is a fascinating study in itself.

Group-Generated Experiences

These are probably among the most common of all religious experiences. We have already looked at the group or religious tradition as a source of personal or mystical experiences, now some elaboration is needed of a point which was made in that discussion, viz.:

(a) *The Influence of Group Expectations.* Very generally speaking, the form the religious experience takes is probably determined by the nature of group expectations. In other words, it is unlikely that the member of a particular religious movement will have a religious experience which is not in keeping with the movement's traditions or which will not meet with its approval.

Examples from two actual movements will show how this operates in practice; firstly, Moral Rearmament, sometimes known simply as MRA or the Oxford Group Movement. It is a Christian movement which has flourished here and in the USA since the early thirties. It may be on the wane now although it did undergo something of a revival in the fifties. It always had a calculated appeal for what are loosely termed the middle-classes; certainly wealth was never any obstacle to membership.

The founder of the movement, Frank Buchman, testified to a very notable religious experience '. . . I realized for the first time the great abyss separating myself from Him [Jesus]. That was all. But it produced in me a vibrant feeling, as though a strong current of life had suddenly been poured into me . . . There was no longer this feeling of a divided will . . . [I had a] new sense of buoyant life . . . [and] a powerful urge to share my experience' [3]. A very similar experience is recorded by a follower of Buchman, A. J. Russell, '. . . I felt an amazing exaltation, an unspeakable rapture, accompanied by a delightful glowing sensation throughout my left side. The ecstasy of this experience is untellable . . . Exactly what happened that day I never quite knew, but I shall always believe that the Creator allowed me to pass a full half-hour on the fringe of Paradise' [4].

Not all participants of the movement laid claims to experiences of quite this intensity, but many insisted that theirs were very similar. The movement encourages a sharing of experiences at its meetings and 'house parties', and the evidence suggests that the recounting of any particular experience tends to differ with the occasion on which it is shared. There may even be a certain amount of 'tailoring' of the description to suit particular audiences.

Few would doubt the sincerity of the people concerned. Some participants testify to dramatic changes in their normal behaviour patterns, but there is a hint that others contrive exaggerated accounts of trivial 'good deeds' in order to impress their fellows. For instance, a shop owner is amazed by what is assumed to be a convert 'who wanted to pay me for a couple of ties he'd swiped two years ago' [5]. A high degree of emotional fervour is often generated at such meetings, and possibly over-elaborated and competitive testimonies follow. Certainly the expectations of the group encourage 'soul-baring' which, though intended to bring a sense of spiritual cleanliness, can degenerate into an uncritical emotionalism.

Secondly, The Pentecostal Movement, which could be described as more an orientation than a movement. It is conservatively Christian in inspiration, and is actually divided into a number of different organizations throughout the world. In general, Pentecostalists believe that the sure sign of an authentic Christian conversion of any individual is that he is 'blessed' with one or more 'gifts of the Spirit'. The gift in question which may be that of prophecy or healing or particularly 'speaking in tongues', is regarded as a validation of that person's salvation. The 'tongues' in question can be actual foreign languages spoken miraculously, that is without previous tuition, in the fashion of the apostles as recorded in the Book of Acts 2. Actual examples of this seem to be rather rare, but such claims are occasionally made. Much more commonly, however, the 'tongue' is said to be a heavenly language apparently referred to by Paul (1 Corinthians 13) when he writes of speaking 'with the tongues of men and of angels'. It is not unusual to hear what sounds like unintelligible rhapsodizing at Pentecostal meetings, with subsequent 'translations' which seem to be identifiably Biblical in tone.

Glossolalia or 'speaking in tongues' in the unintelligible 'language' sense has been a known phenomenon in many parts of the world since remote times. Again, the sincerity of the people concerned is not really in doubt. Although the whole operation is not difficult to simulate or falsify, the believers involved obviously 'feel' that they are speaking an unknown language. Whether they are or not cannot be finally verified one way or the other. What we do know is that in social terms, the phenomenon is used to authenticate the claims of the participants to salvation and special blessing. Newcomers to a group aspire to the same gifts, and almost invariably the expected eventuality becomes the experienced.

One further important point needs to be made. It is the *form* of the experience which is determined by group expectations. This tells us little or nothing about what determines the group expectations themselves, and still less about the sources of religious inspiration. There is some circularity in the reasoning which insists that society somehow produces these in and of itself in order to maintain its own stability [6]. Some experiences may be rather bizarre, and many of the claims unnecessarily extravagant, but underlying them we can surely detect certain common aspirations. Some aspirations will be understandably mundane, the desire for status and respect, the wish to be thought well of by those who lack such experiences. But it can hardly be doubted that some aspirations are for an inner contentment and understanding which are believed to derive from an other-worldly source which is, by definition *supra*-mundane.

Now we must consider a complementary aspect of the group-generated experience, viz.

(b) *The Effects of Group-Emotionalism.* Such effects are very well known in many religious systems, both in primitive and advanced societies. Perhaps we could take two examples which come within our own Judaic-Christian tradition. These will show how potent the effects of emotional arousal can be among certain groups of people.

In the Old Testament scriptures (1 Kings 18), the story is told of the 'contest' between the prophet Elijah and the prophets of Baal. The narrative tells us that Ahab, King of Israel, had married a Phoenician princess, Jezebel (or Jezabaal) who organized the worship of Baal in Israel. This 'imported' religion was served by 450 prophets whom Jezebel supported at her own expense. At Mount Carmel, these are challenged to bring fire to a sacrifice and rain to the land which is suffering from a severe drought. The story is graphically recounted how the prophets work themselves up into an emotional frenzy, cutting themselves with small lances and pleading with Baal to respond to their worship and send fire to the sacrifice. Their fervour is increased by the taunts of Elijah who ridicules their efforts by urging them to scream louder as Baal is obviously asleep.

How accurate are the details of the story, we are not sure, but the whole incident has a certain ring of authenticity. Certainly the religio-political situation in Israel at that time must have been much as the story tells, and the emotional intensity of Baal worship, where people injured themselves unheedingly and worked themselves up into wild sexual frenzies, have their counterparts elsewhere. Such incidents are well known in religious movements such as the Tennessee snake-handling cults and the voodoo cults of Haiti.

In our own times, some people see a resemblance between such scenes as these, and the emotional fervour which is generated at many evangelistic meetings. Some revivalism is not far removed from that of John Wesley and George Whitfield in the eighteenth century. Considerable emphasis was placed upon the wrath of God and upon hell as a place of eternal punishment. Sometimes the results were devastating. 'Hundreds of those present would speak with tongues or bark, display violent jerking, and twitching, while many collapsed senseless on the ground' [7]. Somewhat less emotional scenes were later witnessed at some of the Moody revival meetings during the latter part of the last century, and during the Welsh Revival in the early part of this century.

The much more recent revivalism of Billy Graham during the 1954–5 Evangelistic campaigns, has been much less dramatic, but has displayed certain similar characteristics. The Graham meetings were both highly organized and very successful in relative terms. In an analysis of these campaigns [8], the following points should be noted:

(i) There was an intensive publicity campaign before the meetings began, partly to advertise the event, and partly to boost the prestige of Graham himself. This image-projecting function of the publicity should not be ignored.

(ii) Much use was made of emotional gospel music. The singing was led by a choir of 1,500 and other special soloists. It is important to note here that a much lower number responded at the relay meetings at outside halls, than in the arena itself. (Other experiments have shown that to see and hear is usually more effective than to hear only.)

(iii) The addresses/sermons were given with passion and sincerity. Little stress was put on hell and punishment, but some use was made of the fear of death.

(iv) There were no wild scenes, but it is generally agreed that many people were emotionally moved. Perhaps the fact that applause was forbidden, made the positive act of 'coming out to the front' a means of emotional release.

(v) From various statistics which have been gathered it would appear that over 60 per cent of those who had made 'decisions' and who were not previously church-goers, were still attending church about a year after the campaigns.

The important thing to recognize in all this is the simple fact that like effects need not be attributable to like causes. Emotional arousal of this kind can stem from a number of sources, some of which may have little or nothing to do with religion. Hence, the atmosphere generated at the Nazi Nuremburg rallies in the thirties, or much more recently, the emotional intensity of modern rock concerts have echoes of revival meetings, but are clearly *not* religious meetings at all—certainly not in the strict sense of that term. Further, the needs which give rise to such emotionally charged gatherings need not be causally related to the effects of those gatherings. For instance, it is hardly an act of faith to hope that the effects of a Billy Graham meeting, the conversion of some to the ethic of Jesus, have been quite different from those of a Nazi rally which inculcated the ethics of Aryan superiority and German nationalism. The underlying needs, therefore, of the persons who attended a Nazi rally may have been very similar to those who attended the revival campaign, but the consequences are quite different in each case. What is certainly clear is that both the causes and the effects of revivals and/or conversions cannot be just attributed to mass fervour. To say simply that mass fervour causes anything is really to say nothing at all. Mass fervour itself needs to be explained before it is made the reason for or cause of any social phenomenon. All that can be stated with any empirical certainty is that in particular conditions—some of which can be artificially contrived—similar emotional states can be induced in groups of people (or some people within those groups) which give rise to a variety of effects which might not occur in other circumstances.

Drug-Induced Experiences

These provide a good example of an artificially induced and, therefore, *different* cause which can have a similar effect, viz. that of producing unusual or hallucinatory experiences.

Various peoples have used a number of methods of artificially inducing visions and mystical states, or simply as 'aids' to self-discipline. Yoga exercises, fasting and even self-torture including whipping, have all been used at some time or another in both simple and advanced societies. Religious groups have also made use of drugs for the same purposes. Mescaline, which is derived in its natural state from the peyote cactus, has been used as a stimulant by Mexican tribes for hundreds of years. It may even have been employed in the religious rituals of the Aztecs (see Volume 1).

The effect of the drug varies, but, in general, it produces in the subject a sense of well-being and perhaps even excitement. The person feels relaxed and carefree; and although he also feels that somehow he is sensing some kind of 'reality', experiments show that his thought processes are actually impaired. His sense of time and distance becomes distorted, and hallucinations occur in the form of vivid changing patterns. Sometimes this is accompanied by a sense of self-separation, as though the subject was, and yet was not, himself.

Other drugs can produce similar effects, nitrous oxide and particularly LSD (lysergic acid), and to a much lesser extent, hashish and marijuana. It is understandable that pre-scientific peoples, who had no appreciation of the chemical properties of these drugs, should feel that they were possibly possessed by spirits [9]. It is perhaps less understandable that educated people living in a scientific age, who are to some extent aware of those chemical properties, should still feel that by using drugs of this kind they can be 'introduced' to an otherwise unknown reality.

It is difficult to know to what extent such experiences constitute an 'addition' to the total personality or not. It is not clear whether something 'new' is being induced or generated, or whether the subjects are being enabled by artificial means to realize or express their 'true natures', a notion which would be contested by those 'existentialist' thinkers who insist that the nature of any individual is not set, but changes as it interacts with its environment.

The effect of drugs may be related to the mood or disposition of the subject. It is of some significance that under the influence of drugs, some people still have mystical experiences which conform to their own deeply held beliefs. It is a known phenomenon that some Catholic Mexican peyote users are 'blessed' with Catholic visions [10]. Thus it is possible that experiences derived from drug-taking might be regarded as religious by those involved *if* they already possess a set of religious beliefs with which they can interpret these experiences [11].

This brings us to a crucial point in this whole discussion which is again related to the problem of cause and effect. This is that *the nature of the cause may in no way be related to the form of the effect.* The whipping, the Yoga exercises, the fasting—which may deprive the brain cells of energizing chemicals [12]—and even the drugs may induce experiences, but they cannot determine the form of those experiences.

Or to look at the argument the other way round: an emotion, say fear, may be 'explained' chemically in terms of the discharge of adrenalin which accompanies it. But, in fact, this is no explanation of fear at all—it is simply a description of a process. The adrenalin does not *explain* fear, and it certainly doesn't account of the form fear takes in any particular individual. This is not the province of natural science, but the province of psychology and sociology.

Likewise, with religious experiences. Any attempt to reduce them to a chemical explanation is bound to leave vital questions unanswered. Perhaps some chemical change does take place at the time of such mystical experiences, but it begs the question, did the change precede or merely *accompany* the experience, and if it can be established that it preceded it, can it be deduced that it was causal? After all, A may precede B, but A does not cause B. And none of this begins to tackle the problems of *why* this experience is regarded as religious, and *how* beliefs which interpret the experience come to be held by one and not another.

Similar criticms can be made of attempts to reduce religious experiences to mere psychological phenomena. They are psychological phenomena inasmuch as the mind or psyche is affected, but this does not explain either their nature or their origins. Freud maintained that religious beliefs and experiences simply derive from people's unfulfilled wishes. This view holds that people believe because they want to believe. This has a plausible ring, for undoubtedly some religious practices, for example sacrifice, do arise from the desire to satisfy certain needs. But, yet again, this kind of 'explanation' does not account for either the origins or the nature of certain wishes and desires, particularly for the abstract virtues such as truth, purity, justice and so on.

Inevitably, all these questions are related to the problem of knowledge. How do we know anything? Even the senses through which we are supposed to verify everything are notoriously fallible. For instance, we say 'that man is wearing a blue shirt'. What is really happening in this observation? Light waves are being converted into chemical reactions, chemical reactions are being converted into electricity, and this in turn is then converted into what we interpret as a sensation. But to what extent this sensation corresponds to the 'truth', we have no way of telling. Is the shirt really 'blue', or have our minds somewhow endowed it with the property of blueness? We are not really sure what we see, or hear or touch. The properties we give things are all relative. The table at which you write is only hard and smooth to you; sensitive instruments and honed cutting edges wouldn't 'see' it that way at all.

If experiences must therefore be subject to so many reservations, if our observations are also in question and the seeming 'facts' of everyday life open to dispute, can we presume to be dogmatic about mystical phenomena? To assert that they are 'true' may certainly be presumptuous, but to insist that they are not, may possibly be blind.

3 Haida Indian Totem Pole, Vancouver

Chapter Three

How did religion begin?

Religion is universal. There is no society known to history which has not practised religion in some form or another. Of course, we may not see it this way. We may still find it difficult to associate other ancient, primitive or otherwise unusual religious practices with our own, and be tempted to argue that they are not 'real' religions at all. The worship, say, of crocodile-gods in Ancient Egypt or sacred-cow veneration in modern India seems so remote from our Christian traditions, that we are half-inclined to dismiss them as nonsense, or, at best, as mere superstition. But, as we have seen in Chapter One, insofar as people believe these things, and act on such beliefs, these religious practices are socially 'true', and therefore entitled to our consideration.

Similar criticisms are sometimes made about marriage and the family. What is 'marriage'? Surely any definition of marriage, like that of religion, must have wider connotations than those usually associated with it in the Western mind. Some of our forebears in the last century argued that what passed as marriage in primitive societies was little more than a fiction. The union of one man with several women (polygyny), or the more unusual union of one woman with several men (polyandry) was not altogether unknown to Victorian man. But as new societies were discovered, particularly with the new explorations being made in Central and Southern Africa, stranger and more bizarre marriage forms came to light. Ghost marriage, where a widow cohabits with a man in order to rear children in the name and memory of her dead husband—or his ghost, was found to be quite common in some societies. Woman-to-woman marriage, well known in West Africa, and man-to-man marriage also found among the Indian tribes of British Colombia, were also recognized forms. These were not homosexual unions, but fictive marriages made for economic and alliance purposes, those involved having their own recognized heterosexual partners. Whether these are marriages at all depends entirely upon how the term 'marriage' is defined. As in the case of religion, these practices are universal. Every known society has some form of contractual relationship between the sexes, whether all of these are to be termed 'marriage' is a matter of choice. Primitive peoples, which does not necessarily imply that they are 'simple' or 'savage' but merely non-literate, can be enormously sophisticated in their marriage arrangements. As with their religious practices, these arrangements have their own kind of rationality, they make their own kind of sense. The evidence suggests that, given the conditions existing for those societies, they are, in general terms, suited to the societies in which they are found.

Having established here and in previous discussions a particular position regarding the rationality of religious beliefs and practices, let us now turn to the very puzzling question of origins. *How* religion began is most uncertain. What *is* certain is that no one inventive genius hit upon the idea with the result that it spread throughout the entire world, though obviously some diffusion of ideas about religion has taken place.

Within certain limits, diffusion of ideas has undoubtedly operated in other areas of knowledge besides religion. We know, for example, that the horse-drawn chariot was not in use in the advanced ancient civilizations of Babylonia (modern Iraq) or Egypt until the second millennium BC although the wheel was already well known, and the horse had been domesticated many centuries before by other peoples in the steppes of Asia. Likewise, iron was not successfully smelted, especially for weapons of war, until it was accomplished by the Hittite peoples in Anatolia (modern Turkey) from whence these techniques were diffused throughout the Mediterranean world in the same millennium.

It is sometimes difficult to determine to what extent the appearance of an idea or technique is the result of diffusion or of independent invention. Religion would seem 'originally' to belong to the latter category, as probably no reputable authority would now maintain that it derives from any single source. Thus it might be more meaningful to ask how religions (in the plural) began or how the ideas about religion arose in different societies. But the answers are still only matters of conjecture—still only speculative guesses. The entire business is shrouded in the mists of pre-history about which we really know very little. Dr Eric Waterhouse insists that it cannot *be* answered anymore than the problem of the origins 'of society, of speech, reason, or even precisely, of man himself' [1].

But however speculative our guesses, they can still be intelligent. This reasoned approach to the possible origins of religious beliefs and practices is helped immensely by two other sources of knowledge, namely, anthropology and archaeology. Anthropology is primarily concerned with the study of non-literate peoples who have crafts, but little or no technology. Archaeology, a subject of which the public are far more aware, is concerned with the unearthing of ancient remains, and piecing together the histories of past societies.

Both types of investigation have their limitations, but they complement one another in giving us a clearer picture of how social institutions like religion functioned in antiquity. For instance, archaeologists have discovered what appeared to be toy images among the remains of ancient Greek and Roman houses. These tiny figurines were, in fact, household gods and were part of the ancestor worship of those societies—a practice which has certain affinities with that of keeping religious statuettes in some modern homes. Anthropologists, on the other hand, investigating ancestor worship in modern African societies, e.g. the Lugbara (see Volume 1) have shown how these cults reinforce the dominant role of the senior males within the family group. Only the senior male, that is the eldest surviving male relative of the recently dead ancestor is allowed to have 'contact' with the spirit or ghost of that person; only *he* is permitted to offer sacrifices and only he is believed capable of pleasing the troubled and troublesome spirit. He alone can allay the fear of the spirit, and secure for the family such benefits as health and fertility. This increases his power and authority within the household. In our understanding of the African system, we see more clearly how the senior males, particularly in ancient Rome, found ritual support for their unquestioned authority as family heads; there is evidence that at one period, the father had the power of life and death over his own children. As keeper of the family shrine, he was answerable only to the senior members of his clan where rights and duties were transmitted through the male line.

What have the anthropologists, the archaeologists—and even the psychologists—to say about the possible origins of religious practice? Many theories have been advanced, none of them wholly satisfying. We can look at a few of these, and examine the assumptions that lie behind them.

Ancestor Worship

Herbert Spencer [2], a nineteenth-century sociologist, maintained that in 'using the phrase ancestor worship in its broadest sense as comprehending all worship of the dead . . . we reach the conclusion that ancestor worship is the root of every religion.' Spencer included the kind of ancestor worship already mentioned, and which reached its most complex and elaborate forms in Classical China, i.e. China during the two-thousand-year period prior to the Republican revolution in 1911. He argued, as the Greek writer Euhernerus had done in the third century BC, that worship of the ancestors arose as a form of veneration for dead heroes.

Ancestor worship is not just a matter of respecting the dead. In many societies, it is believed that the ghosts of the dead are responsible for certain mishaps that befall the family or even the tribe—the most important ancestors being those whom tradition teaches were the founders of the tribe. Such spirits must be placated by offerings of corn or wine or even by sacrifices, usually of fowl or other livestock. There is something in this of the notion still held in modern Western societies that ghosts must be pacified, and that restless spirits must be enabled to find their peace.

However, ancient and widespread as ancestor worship undoubtedly is, it can be shown that it is very feebly developed in many of the oldest societies, e.g. Ancient Egypt, and is by no means universal in its distribution. In addition, where it does exist, people almost always clearly differentiate between the ancestor spirits and other deities.

Animism

This theory, which was also strongly advanced in the last century [3], holds that primitive man saw nature as inhabited by a host of nameless spirits associated with various natural objects such as trees, pools and animals. This view is said to derive from the primitives' attempt to grapple with two sets of related biological problems. Firstly, how is it that when we sleep we also dream, and the dream seems to be part of us and yet separate from us? Have we, in some sense, two selves? Are we body *and* spirit (i.e. soul or anima)? And is all nature like this? These questions regarding dreams were also associated with the phenomena of visions, trances and ecstacies when people seem to be 'beside themselves', i.e. someone other than themselves. We have already noted that similar phenomena are experienced with the use and misuse of hallucinatory drugs such as Mescaline and LSD. Secondly, is it possible that we can survive death? If we are both body *and* spirit, has the spirit a separate existence which therefore lives on when the body dies? Does the widespread belief in eternal life stem from this notion of a dual body–soul principle in all nature?

Animism was a very influential theory in its day, and made its mark on a number of eminent nineteenth-century biblical scholars and critics, but today it begs innumerable questions.

The main criticism is that it is no more than a theory. Those who advanced it had insufficient documentary evidence to support it.

Totemism

In some ways this seems to be related to Animism. At least, totemic practices may derive from some animistic ideas. As a theory, it is not so much difficult as strange—particularly to the Western mentality.

There are certain peoples who hold that a special relationship exists between themselves and particular species of animals or plants or perhaps inanimate objects such as rocks or streams. Sometimes even more unlikely objects may be involved like the witchetty grub among the Aborigines of the Arunta country in Australia. The totemic relationship is a ritual one and may be held to exist between the individual, the family, a clan or tribe, or possibly some other kind of group and the natural object.

Totemism takes a great variety of forms, even within limited areas. For example, the group may be forbidden to kill the totem animal, or in other cases, it may be expressly enjoined to do so. In Melanesia, certain birds are regarded as totemically sacred, and no one is allowed to hunt them. On the other hand, Aborigine peoples will hunt and kill kangaroos despite the fact that they are regarded as totem animals. It obviously pays to protect, to some extent, the creatures on whom you depend, thus some Siberian tribes venerate bears, but nevertheless kill them—with 'apologies'—because they need to, but take great care to look after their young. The women of the tribe sometimes even suckle the cubs by way of compensation.

The three main proponents of totemism as the starting-point of all religions were W. Robertson Smith [4], a minister of religion who saw in the killing and eating of the totem animal the root idea of the Christian Communion Service; the influential psychologist Sigmund Freud [5]; and the not popularly known but very important sociologist, Emile Durkheim [6].

As with ancestor worship, the main general criticism of this theory is that it simply does not fit all the facts. Totemism is by no means either universally or evenly distributed throughout the globe, in fact, totemism is a blanket term in that it is used to cover a multitude of sometimes similar but often widely differing practices in primitive religions.

Assumptions and Criticisms

There are specific criticisms which could be levelled at each of these theories, but the following are some very general criticisms which apply to all three.

(i) There is, as has already been suggested, a general lack of evidence for these theories. Ethnographies of primitive peoples, i.e. detailed studies of those peoples and their ways of life by trained observers, were still in their infancy when these theories were first advanced and popularized. Many theorists were not themselves eye-witnesses of these societies, but took their material at second-hand from travellers, missionaries and early anthropologists who had recorded their findings; this is certainly true of Spencer, Freud and Durkheim.

(ii) Then there is the matter of making the facts fit the case. In this, theorists sometimes resorted to procrustean techniques. Procrustes, some of you will recall, was an extremely hospitable person in Greek mythology. The snag was that he could only offer a bed of a particular size, and guests who were too short for it had to have their legs stretched, and those who were too long had to have their legs cut off. Some theorists have been like this. They have had inspired ideas and developed interesting theories to account for known phenomena—but they often attempted to make as much of the evidence as they could fit the theories. Where it would not fit, they sometimes tended to discount it.

(iii) There is also what may be called the 'reading back' problem. This consists of trying to imagine what others would have done in particular circumstances, in this case, why would primitives worship in the ways that they do? (It's like a parent wanting to buy a child a present and asking not 'What would he like?', but 'What would *I* like if I were that age?') It's so easy to make the wrong guess, when real evidence is lacking. We can only conjecture as to why people have thought it right and necessary to worship in the ways they have. To us, human sacrifice (as we saw in Volume 1) may seem senseless and cruel, but often the people who practised it were not particularly cruel, and it made a certain kind of sense to them. It should be clear that we can never 'see' it as they did, nor completely understand their motives. Their rationales for such practices were developed in societies quite foreign to us, and any theories we can offer as to their motives must be mere 'intellectualizations' of the situations.

(iv) Lastly, there is the 'stages' problem. This is really a criticism of an assumption made by some earlier writers. Towards the end of the last century—and these attitudes still survive today—Europeans, particularly, tended to believe that the world's peoples could be classified not only on the basis of their technology or lack of it, but also according to certain social practices. For example, if a society was polygamous (as historically most societies have been), i.e. having marriage forms where one person was joined to several partners, it was generally thought to be 'uncivilized'. If, on the other hand, it was monagamous, i.e. where one person is joined to one partner only, this was thought to be a characteristic of a higher state or 'stage' of civilization.

Similarly with religion. If a people had many gods, they were thought to be at a lower 'stage' of development compared with those who worshipped one god only. The latter were held to be more truly religious, and at a 'high stage' of human development.

Any examination of 'lower' and 'higher' peoples fails to prove conclusively that this is the case. Even primitives, who are expected to think of Europeans as civilized, hesitate when they are told that these same Europeans have butchered over fifty millions of their fellows in two world wars. They might well question whether Europeans have the right to set the standards, and indeed whether Europeans live up to the standards they set.

This tendency to think of one's own people as being right, or at least 'more right' than others is technically called ethnocentricity, and literally means that one's own race or people are always to be regarded as central and most important. Many societies have been guilty of this in their time. It is an extremely ancient form of prejudice, both the Chinese and the Greeks once thought of everyone outside their borders as 'barbarians' (in Greek, literally 'strangers' or 'foreigners'). In more recent times, we have had the Nazis with their myth of the Aryan peoples who were supposedly superior to all others; there was never any evidence to support this view. To be fair, in this matter of enthnocentricity, the British have not been entirely innocent, but no one has taken it to such lengths as the Germans between 1933 and 1945.

Conclusions

We have seen then that such theories as ancestor worship, animism and totemism (and there are others) as the 'original' religions cannot be upheld by the facts. They are sometimes called 'simplistic' explanations because they adopt a short-cut approach which ignores unpleasant exceptions to the rule. In effect, they are theories which tend to discount the primacy of belief and stress instead religious experience and practice. Beliefs are seen rather as intellectualizations of experience and practice; a series of theoretical after-thoughts which attempt to explain them.

A more meaningful way of approaching this problem is to ask what possible causes are likely to produce religious beliefs and practices as their effect? After all, looked at 'from a distance', as it were, religion is a rather strange business. For what reasons are humans likely to people the universe with unseen but superior beings who control the destinies of men and who influence human affairs?

Religion and Economic Necessity

One factor which may well have given rise to certain kinds of religious belief and practice, is the simple one of trying to secure an adequate food supply. Scarcity was normal. For most of history, men have eked out a very precarious existence, relying first on edible fruits and roots, and later on simple cultivation. Much of the time, they have literally scratched a living from the soil. They must have asked themselves if there were any ways in which they could guard against the uncertainties of nature. Indeed, the world of nature must have seemed harsh and unpredictable, and at times downright hostile. Could one take out some kind of insurance against disease? Was there a way of ensuring good crops and healthy herds? Surely these things were controlled by powerful, invisible beings who must be open to a well-intentioned approach? Perhaps an 'arrangement' could be made with these gods, and what better arrangement than that of some form of gift-exchange. It worked among men, why not between men and the unseen powers? But discussion with the gods is not possible, one must guess at the sort of things that would please them. Perhaps some return of the things they granted in the first place, wheat, oil and wine—and even life itself? Possibly sacrifices began this way; many societies have festivals of the 'firstfruits' as a thanksgiving to the gods. This is all rather hypothetical, but not unreasonably so considering the 'findings' of anthropologists working with current primitive societies.

Very generally speaking, primitive societies can be divided into:

Nomadic peoples, where small groups make their way from water-hole to water-hole in desert or arid country, e.g. Bedouin Arabs, or the Bushmen of the Kalahari Desert in South West Africa.

Hunting and fishing peoples, e.g. the Plains Indians (Sioux, Cheyenne, etc.) of central United States and the Blackfeet tribes of Canada.

Simple pastoralists, those who wander with their herds within a limited area, and do some hunting as well, e.g. the Nuer and Dinka of the Sudan, or the Masai of Kenya.

Cultivators, more settled groups who cultivate, often in river valleys, maize, barley, wheat, rice, etc.

Without doubt, early societies fell into similar categories, and religion took different forms according to the type of society in which it was found. It is interesting to look at some examples of these practices, and relate them to this whole question of economic necessity.

Hunting ritual. At Lescaux and Carnac, and at other sites in or near the Pyrenees, there are cave-paintings dating from the Upper Paleolithic Period, i.e. from about 40,000 to about 10,000 years ago. These paintings represent stags, reindeer, bison and horses being pierced by arrows. What were the reasons for these scenes in the caves? Or were there no particular reasons, were they merely the pastimes of some very early artists? No one is quite sure but it seems that the likelihood is that they were possibly painted as part of some kind of hunting ritual.

Quite possibly, they were not, for the artist, a record of a past event, but an impression of something which he and his companions hoped was going to happen in the near future. Perhaps the painting was made in order to influence the mysterious forces in order to secure success in the hunt that was about to take place. At the same time, the ritual which accompanied it acted as a psychological 'spur' to the hunters and increased both their courage and their confidence for the chase.

This, of course, was the main purpose of the war dances which were a common feature of many primitive societies. Among the Zulu, for example, in the last century, the 'art' of 'doctoring' the warriors was practised by witchdoctors. This consisted of rituals which were designed to protect the warriors against enemy spears. It was even believed by some during the Zulu Wars that they would be impervious to the white man's bullets which would turn to water. At least, this was the supposed function of the rituals, their actual function was to bolster the Zulu morale for battle.

Fertility ritual. This was largely confined to pastoralists and

4 Diana at Ephesus

cultivators [7]. Among the cultivator societies, rituals were often quite elaborate. They lived in relatively settled communities, and by comparison with hunters and pastoralists, were quite prosperous. In fact, they were often able to produce a surplus which enabled them to pay some of their number to specialize in certain crafts such as pottery, brick work, weaving, weapon-making—and, not least of all, priestcraft. It was the priest's task to please the gods in order that the prosperity might continue. Religion was really a kind of mutual back-scratching arrangement between men and the gods. And it flourished because fertility was vital.

Fertility rituals took many forms, some of which would be regarded as shocking today—even though modern society has its own particular brands of absurdity and obscenity. Some very ancient figurines have been found in Europe, the most famous of which was found in Austria and given the unlikely name of the 'Venus of Willendorf'. They are extremely crude, and almost without exception show heavily pregnant women with large breasts. In fact, these are really their only features. How, or even whether, they were worshipped is quite unknown to us; but almost certainly they had some kind of fertility function.

Or again, in the New Testament (Acts 19: 35) reference is made to 'Diana of the Ephesians'; this is a mistake. The goddess in question was in fact a Greek deity, Artemis, who was worshipped over much of the Middle East. At Ephesus (in modern Turkey) she was worshipped as Artemis Polymastos (the many-breasted). She was depicted in female form but covered in breasts; these, of course, were meant to symbolize her fertile, mother-like qualities.

The 'Great Mother' image as a symbol of sympathy and fertility has been worshipped since pre-historic times under various names, and in various guises. Indeed, it has been argued with some force that the high regard for the Virgin Mary mainly among Roman Catholics is a 'purified' legacy of this.

Associated with fertility worship was often the practice of

ritual intercourse. In ancient Babylonia, the king and his consort were expected on the appropriate occasion, to lead a procession up the giant Ziggurat, which was very much like a flat-topped pyramid, but with stairs and terraces, and either there or in a small temple enclosure, to have sexual intercourse as part of the ritual. This act, obviously associated with the whole idea of fertility, was believed to ensure benefits from the gods for the people.

Ritual intercourse was extremely common in ancient times throughout the Middle East, and particularly in Syria, the Lebanon and Israel; there are several criticisms of it in the Old Testament. Those who participated in these acts presumably saw themselves as being in harmony with the natural order of things. It was a symbolic act. They were merely simulating nature itself which brings fruit from the womb of the earth.

In some parts of the world, notably India, these practices have continued until quite modern times. In India, it took the form of temple prostitution. Young girls were either given or sold to the temples; here they acted as prostitutes for customers who paid the priests for the privilege. It is quite likely that this was a degenerate form of fertility ritual, which served a more direct economic purpose—the money was used for the upkeep of the temple and its priests.

Despite the overwhelming evidence of a correspondence between economic need and religious observances, there is also ample proof that societies will commit forms of economic 'suicide' for ritual purposes. For instance, the Tikopia, an island people in the Pacific, traditionally burnt canoes on the death of a chief. The gravity of this act can only be appreciated if one realizes how valuable a canoe is to this people who live mainly by fishing. In economic terms, this represents a piece of 'capital equipment' (like a cargo ship or a railway train would be to us) which it seems pointless to destroy—but ritual is not necessarily rational.

Similarly, the Hindu reverence for cows appears idiotic to the Westerner. With so much scarcity in India, and the ever present hunger of so many people, where in 1943 over a million people died in Bengal province alone of starvation, it seems completely nonsensical to preserve innumerable, often mangy, cows who can roam virtually anywhere at will. As Raymond Firth puts it, 'the Brahmanic bull of Hindu India swings through the bazaar and eats his fill; the European sees in him a wasteful concession to religious prejudice, and thinks how much better he would be occupied in pulling a plough or converted into steaks' [8]. But this is part of the Hindu faith. They eat no beef, as Muslims eat no pork. To a people like ourselves who are accustomed to gorging ourselves on Sunday joints, the whole idea of bloodless sacrifices makes little sense, but this is a very deeply ingrained aspect of Hindu tradition.

What is clear from the evidence, is that all people do not always put economic necessity first, although it is—and must be—among men's primary considerations. It could be argued that ritual has its own kind of economic rationality in that if the rituals were not performed at extreme cost, the people concerned might believe they would suffer even greater economic deprivation at the hands of the gods. But such explanations do not take account of other reasons for religious observances.

Religion as a Product of Fear

The ancients had a saying that 'fear made the gods'. The strength of this argument is that it is obviously true, the weakness of the argument is that it is equally obviously only part of the truth. Pre-scientific man must have feared the natural forces outside his control. What were those lights in the sky which blinked at the earth and often seemed to disappear unpredictably? Were they gods? What of the thunderous noises from dark clouds, the streaks of light which seemed to split the heavens. Were the gods angry?

These things were beyond the primitive's understanding, and they added to the uncertainties of his existence. If he could, he must come to terms with them—he must allow for every possibility. Thus certain Polynesian peoples in their island home would try to ensure favour of these supernatural forces by sacrificing to the gods of the local, active volcano in order to prevent its eruption. Humans were fed into its ugly mouth to satisfy and pacify it.

Fear takes many forms: fear of the unpredictable, fear of beasts, fear of ghosts, fear of enemies—fear of the certainty of death. Is religion then merely a form of fear? Different kinds of fear have to be allayed in different ways. Fear in itself usually leads to flight—to retreat. Religion is more than this; ritual is a form of approach. If religion is no more than fear, one could assume that when the danger is past, ritual should die away. It does *change*, but it remains to a lesser or greater degree a perennial activity in all societies. In religion, the sentiments are not easy to isolate, but they certainly include wonder, admiration and awe, besides fear. Fear may well be *one* ingredient in the religious impulse—but there are certainly others. Fear, as an explanation, does not take account of all the facts.

The Common Features of Religion

Religion everywhere involves a sense of the 'beyond'—a sense of the sacred. Sometimes this is associated with places, for example, Jacob at Bethel awakes from a dream and says, 'How dreadful is this place . . . Yahweh is here and I did not realize it' (Genesis 28: 10–22). At other times, it is associated with people: the writer of the Gospel of John speaks of Jesus as 'that one', i.e. the strange or other one—not one of us—the one from 'there', the one from 'beyond'.

In some cases, the 'sacred' may be applied to objects such as sacred relics or maybe to something like a ritual law of a tribe. The object may be worthless in itself, and the law may seem to be of no real significance, but they are *given* qualities, they are endowed with properties that they do not demonstrably possess, and which cannot be verified by experimentation. They are 'other'; they may be set aside or sanctified and regarded with special veneration. Just a brief reflection will show that such attitudes and practices are by no means confined to ancient or primitive societies. In our own society, they apply to such things as consecrated church buildings, to Communion bread and wine, to the water of baptism—even to the people whom we call priests. None of these self-evidently possess the qualities assigned to them, but the beliefs persist.

The sacred may be surrounded by a 'taboo', it must not be violated or harmed in any way. For example, in the Old Testament we find the death of some youths attributed to the fact that they abused the prophet Elisha, a man of God, and therefore, by definition, a sacred person. It may even be believed that some kind of curse attaches to an object, for instance, the three-thousand-year-old Tomb of Tutankhamun found virtually intact in Egypt. This idea has found some support from the fact that many people associated with the excavation of this tomb in 1922 have died under rather unusual circumstances.

In the 'higher religions', the 'sacred' is very closely connected not so much with objects as *objectives*. It is not *just* a product either of fear or economic necessity, but an idealistic attempt to invest life with meaning and purpose and direction. The Japanese religion of Shinto is called 'the way of the gods'; the Buddhist faith teaches 'the noble eight-fold path'; early Christianity was simply called 'the Way'. These suggest that religion is a kind of movement, a striving to attain certain goals. An often solitary, but courageous endeavour.

5 An Inquisition scene at Goa in the seventeenth century

Chapter Four

How can religion be analysed?

Academics have suggested a number of ways of categorizing religious systems. In Volume 1, a reasonably simple division of four types was given: family religions, tribal religions, state religions, universal religions. This division was useful within certain limits; it involved a certain amount of overlapping, but this is inevitable with any attempt at categorization. In reality, religious systems do not slot neatly into convenient conceptual pigeon-holes.

A somewhat different analysis which is rather more sociologically sophisticated will be used for our present discussion, namely, a three-fold division of religious systems into:

1. WORLD-REJECTING SYSTEMS
2. WORLD-ACCEPTING SYSTEMS
3. WORLD-TRANSFORMING SYSTEMS.

This scheme is open to similar objections, but it does have the virtue of being an analysis as opposed to a mere description of types. It is an attempt to look at religious systems in terms of their functions, and these functions are seen in relation to, or as a reaction against what is termed the 'world'. Now this is not an easily defined concept, but it does connote the secular rather than the sacred, the human values which are conditioned by material and physical considerations rather than spiritual ideals and aspirations. Obviously, in practice, one impinges upon the other, so that, for example, some people express those spiritual aspirations in physical ways; in music or in art and architecture, or in 'good deeds' which may be both self-denying and self-enhancing.

Another point which must be made about this kind of

analysis is that the categories used are only *constructs*. That is to say, they are simply models which are used for the sake of convenience. No religious system is completely world-rejecting or completely world-accepting. Actual religious systems only approximate to one category or another, but by constructing models we can, in a sense, 'measure' the extent or otherwise of conformity of actual systems in relation to the model. Or, to put it another way, we are trying to discover the degree of correspondence between actual religious systems and an 'ideal type' of system which is really only a theoretical construct. After all, when we measure or weigh anything, we are only applying the same principle. Both the item measured and the measure itself have no objective validity. There are no actual metres or litres; all measurement is relative and simply a matter of convenience.

I. WORLD-REJECTING SYSTEMS

As a *type*, world-rejecting systems are very much minority systems with certain well-defined characteristics:

(i) They tend to comprise relatively small tightly knit groups of the type usually referred to as 'sects'.

(ii) The members may be largely—but by no means wholly—those who are rather loosely termed 'underprivileged'. This can refer to 'status deprivation', i.e. a relative lack of esteem in the society of which they are a part. But it more usually denotes forms of social deprivation which are primarily political and economic.

(iii) They can be—and sometimes are—persecuted groups.

(iv) They are, by definition, separatist groups in the sense that although members are active in the world of commerce and industry, they try to divorce themselves from certain of its values. In New Testament terminology, they are 'in the world but not of it'.

(v) Alternatively, they may be isolationist to the extent that they live and work in spatially separate communities.

(vi) They are usually breakaway movements from a larger, more inclusive, religious tradition. For example, there are many such groups within the general Christian tradition, although certain more orthodox Christians might deny their right to inclusion.

(vii) In doctrine, they will almost certainly lay stress on some particular aspect of belief which is not greatly emphasized among the more orthodox, e.g. prophecy or healing. In fact, this may well be their *raison d'être*—their main reason for a separate existence as a group.

(viii) One belief which probably characterizes most of such movements is the underlying conviction that the world is either positively evil, and therefore irredeemable, or, at best, something which can be discounted as a mere stepping-stone to a more perfect and eternal reality. To this extent they may be 'chiliastic' in that they work for the destruction of this 'world order' and the ushering in of the next.

(ix) The organization of these movements cannot really be seen as a type, since they take a variety of very different forms. They may be loosely organized on a democratic (a perhaps, in theory, theocratic or god-ruled) basis. They may be hierarchically organized with various levels of authority, or even autocratically organized around a single leader.

(x) They are often 'total' systems in that they tend to regulate the whole lives of their members.

(xi) Normally, their members are bound by a comparatively strict moral code.

To see how nearly this composite model corresponds with actuality, it might be as well to compare two such movements, one of which might be very generally regarded as separatist, and the other as isolationist.

Jehovah's Witnesses. This movement, sometimes known as The Watchtower Bible and Tract Society, had its origins in the USA about 1879. The members of the movement believe that they are the latest—perhaps even the last—of a long line of witnesses of Jehovah God (Jehovah being a form of the Hebrew sacred name for God) extending from Abel the son of Adam until the present day. Their view is that Jesus, as God's special creation is the head of a spiritual kingdom of 144,000 members among whom they trust they are numbered.

Although the Witnesses are pacifistic, they look forward to a triumph in the 'last battle' called Har-maggedon between the forces of Jehovah and the forces of Satan (evil), when the earth will become the idyllic home for the survivors and for many others who will be raised from the dead. There is some dispute over the detail [1], and particularly the timing of the fulfilment of prophecy. There have been 'postponements', but the latest date has a familiar ring—1984.

Jehovah's Witnesses are keenly evangelistic, and try to spread their doctrines through booklets and house-to-house visitation. They are particularly intent on maintaining the faith within the family unit. But in all this, they are separatist in the sense that they adopt values and practices which, rightly or wrongly, have marked them off from most other members of society. They are almost pathologically critical of the orthodox Churches and refuse to observe many of their teachings and festivals—even Christmas. They tend also to be anti-science, and may take unfavourable views of modern medicine and education. Their extreme pacifism and non-co-operation with authority has made them clear targets under certain dictatorships, particularly in Nazi Germany. Their dogmatism, which, in a favourable setting, sometimes leads to ridicule, has, in other circumstances, marked them out as people of courage and determination.

The Shakers. This movement, an example of a more isolationist group, is also associated with the USA, although it actually began in England in the eighteenth century as an offschoot of Quakerism (The Society of Friends). The term 'shaker' is really derisive and refers to the convulsions and ecstasies which are encouraged in the worshippers. The official title of the movement is the United Society of Believers in Christ's Second Coming.

The first Shaker settlement was near Albany in New York State. Other settlements were formed as a result of the missionary enthusiasm of the early converts. They flourished in the difficult days of pioneer America, but today are said to number no more than about a hundred members in five separate communities, despite the early belief that they would increase in members until the time of the Second Advent of Christ, when the Earth would be 'reborn'.

Their beliefs constitute a very unorthodox kind of Christianity. The essential difference is the notion that God is dual, comprising both an Eternal Father and an Eternal Mother. They accept the revelation of Jesus, but reject the theory of an atoning death. In addition, they acknowledge the revelation of their founder, Mother Ann Lee as the 'Bride of the Lamb', a kind of feminine Messiah.

Traditionally, the Shakers were organized in separate communities. They had no priests or paid ministry although there were Elders and Elderesses; they employed no doctors and refused medicine. They were celibate and repudiated what they regarded as 'carnal sexual indulgence'. They drew their strength from the recruitment of new converts, and welcomed married couples providing they lived as 'brothers and sisters'. The children of such couples were carefully educated within the community. There was no discrimination of sex, of race, or religion; Jews and Negroes were all of equal rank within the settlement. But all were expected to abide by the strict rules of the community. They had a reputation for honesty and hard work, in fact, labour was regarded as a sacred duty —a rather necessary belief among small, poor co-operatives of farmers. They were also extremely pacifistic, denouncing war and, in general, leading chaste and temperate lives.

Perhaps it is significant that their greatest loss of membership has taken place in the last hundred years, a period in which advances in technology and science have been hastening the end of small agricultural communities in Western societies.

Except for Monastic Orders, very few separatist groups now flourish, although many still exist. These are composed mainly of people who have grown disillusioned with the world and its values, and have sought refuge among the like-minded, often in isolated communities. Sometimes these groups are characterized by specific religious beliefs, but these are no longer considered necessary as justifications for a separate existence.

2. WORLD-ACCEPTING SYSTEMS

Of course, *all* religious systems 'accept' the world to some extent. World-accepting systems, as a type, simply tend to accept it more than others. The main characteristics of such systems are that:

(i) They are usually large, inclusive, and even relatively popular religious systems. Within Christianity, the Church of England would be a good example.

(ii) They are rarely persecuted because their values are not necessarily at variance with those of the surrounding society. In more sociological terms, they are increasingly 'accommodating' to the world, and little or no 'tension' exists between them and society at large.

(iii) They tend to give rise—indirectly—to breakaway movements whose members despair of the accommodation process, and who therefore try to recapture something of the purity of the 'original' faith—whatever that may be.

(iv) They tend to increase their memberships by birth rather than by conversion. People are simply born into a system, which they may never seriously question.

(v) By definition, they do not necessarily regard the world as evil, but as an extension of the realm of god or the gods.

(vi) Like world-rejecting systems, they may be organized in a number of different ways, although usually there is some kind of developed authority structure.

(vii) They adopt liberal attitudes towards moral issues.

Very generally speaking, world-accepting systems can be divided for convenience into two types which can be called the accommodating and the endorsing types.

The Accommodating System. In its formative years this system may well have had stricter and more rigid views. Indeed, at one time, it may have even been world-rejecting in emphasis, but time and circumstances have eroded its original outlook and intentions. It has gradually surrendered these, and come to terms with the world whose values it once disputed, if not actually despised—a process known technically as 'secularization'. This secularization process—in one form or another—has taken place throughout most of the world. All the great religious systems, Hinduism, Buddhism, Judaism, Christianity, Islam, etc., have to a greater or lesser extent proved accommodating, particularly in the wake of increasing industrialization in the countries concerned. Certain branches of these faiths have held out, but by and large for the systems as a whole, it has meant considerable change. Whether this change is to be welcomed depends very much upon the perspective of the observer; there are certainly those who look upon the process as one of actual decline.

These changes take place in response to the varied pressures in the modern world. These, of course, have particularly affected Christianity, and few movements have been able to withstand these pressures. The effects of such pressures on these movements can probably best be seen in their economic arrangements and their changing attitudes towards many moral issues.

The financing of modern religious organizations has apparently necessitated the direct involvement of those organizations in certain areas of business. Religious groups such as the Baptists or, more particularly, the Salvation Army, which in their early formative years would have eschewed the whole idea of business investments, have now become enmeshed in the commercial world. Not only have they shareholdings in commerce and industry (and at a time when the investor can rarely be exactly sure as to the nature of those businesses), but as organizations they are now run and financed as business enterprises with their own Pension Funds and Insurance schemes. Changes of attitude are even more obvious in relation to a number of ethical problems (as we noted in Volume 1). The moral 'stance' of some religious groups has been modified; in fact, a process of liberalization is undoubtedly still taking place.

The Quakers (Society of Friends) are a case in point. As a movement, they date from the seventeenth century. In their early days, they were noted for certain eccentricities of dress and behaviour. Their codes were strict and their attitudes unyielding. They denounced war and refused to take oaths; and during the seventeenth century thousands were goaled for their beliefs and practices. In fact, in the early colonial years in the United States, some were hanged and others were suspected of witchcraft and forced to leave the country.

All this has changed. Quaker dress is no longer seen, and characteristic Quaker use of 'thee' and 'thou' is now rarely, if ever, heard. But these are understandable departures from traditional practice. What is more difficult to appreciate are the relaxed attitudes on issues which were once subject to strict prohibitions.

Originally, membership had been allowed on profession of faith, but by as early as the eighteenth century Quakers' children were being admitted as birth-members. With increasing prosperity, the nature of the movement began to change, it came to include well-to-do bankers, merchants and the like. There is evidence to show that as time passed, 'wealth and length of Quaker descent became valued sources of status within Quakerism . . . Friends were coming to accept the values of their environment, and respect for worldly rank and titles was often mentioned as one of their characteristics' [2].

In the early part of the nineteenth century, we find that such diversions as dancing had been proscribed, and 'novels, the theatre, and all games of chance (had) been forbidden' [3]. 'Doubtful' pictures were also condemned, and teetotalism was general throughout the movement. Although Quakerism preached a doctrine of toleration, and in general encouraged serious pursuits, it feared 'worldly attachment' and what it regarded as intellectual pride.

By and large, these views are no longer held by Quakers, although there are, of course, some exceptions to this. Opinions have changed, and broader interpretations of New Testament teaching are now in vogue. The stress is on the authority of the individual conscience rather than the authority of the movement to decide what members should or should not do. The relatively recent 'Towards a Quaker View of Sex' with its tendencies towards a certain uncharacteristic permissiveness, bears this out. And what has been said about Quakerism is, in general, reflected in the development—or decline—of many other Christian bodies. World-rejecting systems sometimes capitulate to pressure of opinion and become world-accepting systems.

The Endorsing System. This is quite different in its development if not in its attitudes. Unlike the accommodating system, it has never had any very serious quarrel with the world and its values, indeed, it tends to endorse and defend them. From the outset, it is liberal and 'humanistic' in its outlook. Only one world faith, as such, comes into this category, Confucianism—and then only in a qualified sense—for some people would argue that this isn't really a faith at all, but a kind of tolerant ethical philosophy. There are strong endorsing elements in other world faiths, particularly Christianity, so we will subsequently look at one of these, the Unitarian movement.

Confucianism derives its name though not *all* its teachings from K'ung Fu-Tzu (latinized form, Confucius) who is said to have been born in 551 BC in Shantung province. He served as an adviser and teacher at a number of different courts in pre-classical China. Strictly speaking, he was not a religious teacher but a moralist. He tended to accept the religious systems of his day which were mainly forms of ancestor worship, and instructed his pupils that these ritual practices were among their principal obligations.

Primarily, Confucianism is concerned with the balanced life, and the practice of moderation in all things. It inculcated the spirit of filial piety and respect for elders and superiors, and prescribed very specific rules of behaviour within the family. It was essentially conservative in that in its hey-day, in the China of pre-1911 AD, it was concerned to preserve traditional values and age-old virtues.

Confucianism is—or perhaps more strictly was—an endorsing system insofar as it tended to support current morality and encourage established practices. It accepted the world of which it was a part, and even provided justifications for the existing social order.

Unitarianism, on the other hand, is somewhat different. As a movement which developed in sixteenth-century Europe within the general ambit of Christianity, it positively welcomed new thinking on every conceivable issue. It was tolerant and liberal from the beginning, and led the way in radical religious thinking until well into the last century.

Unitarians became best known for their unorthodox views about the Trinity. They hold that God is a unity (hence the term, Unitarian) and not three Persons in One, the Trinitarian position. Actually, this is only one facet of their teaching.

The basis of Unitarianism is really a belief in the essential goodness of man, and in his capacity for self-improvement. They repudiate all creeds and statements of dogmatic belief, and argue that individuals are capable of interpreting spiritual and moral issues for themselves. Unitarians are extremely tolerant of other world religions to the extent that they are one of the few Christian bodies who have no overseas missionary societies. This open-mindedness has led many of them to a position which is little short of agnosticism, an almost paralysing uncertainty about virtually every theological issue. Indeed, it can be argued that it is this very open-mindedness which has been a major cause of their comparative decline in recent years. It would appear that in religious matters, those with a *positive* message flourish, whilst those—like the Unitarians—who are very liberal in their thinking, tend to fade into obscurity.

3. WORLD-TRANSFORMING SYSTEMS

Again it is necessary to stress the fact that these categories are conceptual, and in a sense a little artificial when related to actual religious systems. No system is completely world-transforming, but this idea does express one of the primary features of some religious movements. The world-transforming system shares many characteristics with both the other categories. In fact, in one sense, it is a kind of synthesis of the others. It tends to be strict in its moral requirements and dogmatic in its doctrines. A state of tension exists between it and the surrounding society. This it has in common with world-rejecting systems.

On the other hand, membership may either be by birth or conversion, and the organization of such systems can take a variety of forms. The particular features of such systems, particularly in the Judao–Christian–Islamic tradition, are that:

(i) The world may be regarded as evil, but it is not irredeemably evil. Men are believed to be capable of change. But it is just here that the movements divide. Some hold that *all* men can be saved, or even *will be* saved, whilst others maintain that this is a privilege reserved only for a chosen few—a favoured 'elect'.

(ii) The movement has a distinctive 'message' which must be proclaimed. All other religious systems are either regarded as completely wrong or, at best, not as right as the particular movement in question.

(iii) The 'message' is carried by members and/or professional evangelists and representatives who are dedicated to the cause of either world-wide proclamation, e.g. the Christian W.E.C. organization (the World Evangelization Crusade) or to the conversion of specific peoples or communities, e.g. the Christian Mission to the Jews.

(iv) This 'message' may either be spread by proclamation and persuasion, or by conquest and coercion.

From what has been said, it is obvious that world-transforming systems can be distinguished in a number of ways. For the sake of simplicity in the present discussion, another two-fold division is proposed on the basis of (iv), the distinction between evangelical and militant movements. Our examples will be taken from Christianity and Islam.

It should be emphasized, however, that neither of these world faiths has been *entirely* evangelical or militant, although certain movements within them, especially Christianity, have been entirely non-militant, e.g. the Methodists. Evangelicalism (used now in a special sense) and militancy have been characteristics of both religions at different periods in their histories and at different stages in their development.

Evangelicalism is probably best illustrated from Christianity simply because its 'good news' or evangel is, by definition, something which must be proclaimed. Admittedly, there are many ways of doing this. The model way, so to speak, has been for small bands of dedicated believers to organize themselves in ways which will promote and sustain missionary endeavour. This was the pattern laid down from the earliest days by Paul and the original apostles (the literal N.T. Greek meaning, 'those which are sent'). In the main, this model has been followed by subsequent missionary movements, which have tried by persuasion and example to convert their hearers.

The rise of modern missionary movements from the end of the eighteenth century has meant series of somewhat mixed blessings for the recipients. The missionary efforts of various societies may have involved unacceptable strictures on such traditional tribal practices as polygamy, certain fertility rituals and cliterodectomy (female circumcision) in Africa. But it has also helped to eradicate suttee (the practice of burning a widow on the funeral pyre of her late husband) in India, and to suppress headhunting in Sarawak. Missionary endeavour has brought attendant benefits, particularly educational and medical facilities to those who sorely needed them. But it has also brought trails of colonizers, traders and the like who were prepared to exploit the native, plus a whole host of new and highly infectious diseases from which vast numbers have perished.

Some anthropologists paint an idyllic picture of native societies before the advent of the missionaries, and tend to favour the idea that these societies would have been better left alone. On the other hand, the journals of early travellers often describe darker sides to some of these societies [4], starvation, slaving, human sacrifice, despotism and arbitrary executions, which show that life was not quite as rosy as some would have us think. Although on the debit side, the fate of some of these peoples at the hands of unscrupulous conquerors and colonizers defies description. To take just one particularly bad period of about 150 years in Africa alone, it is estimated that some twenty million natives died [5] as the result of the slave trade which reached its height in the early nineteenth century. The evils of slaving were not directly connected with the evangelical efforts of the missionaries but were one of the concomitants of the opening of new territories. The missionaries sometimes overlooked these evils, but often—as in the case of David Livingstone—they spent much of their time trying to eradicate them.

Evangelical systems are essentially those which see others as those in need of 'salvation'. They may promote educational and medical schemes for the relief of temporary or local distress, but by and large, they have no large-scale political or social aims. The radical political view is that individuals will only change when society itself is changed, either by legislative or revolutionary action. The evangelicals, on the other hand, have a predominantly spiritual message which is addressed to the individual. It is central to the evangelical mentality that societies can only change for the better when the individuals which comprise them are changed. As the apostle Paul put it, 'Do not be conformed to this world, but be transformed by the renewing of your minds. . . .'

Militancy has been a characteristic of many systems, but it is particularly linked with Islam and some forms of Christianity. In Islam, the religion of Muhammad, violence was at first forbidden, and conversion was to be accomplished by persuasion. But very early on, even during the lifetime of the Prophet, we find convenient 'revelations' which not only permit but also urge the use of force to compel submission. The basic creed was simply 'There is no God but Allah, and Muhammad is His Prophet'. Unbelievers were offered the chance to accept Islam (the word actually implies submission), but if they refused, the Faithful had a duty to compel the hesitant and slay the recalcitrant. In AD 625, Muhammad and his followers began to eliminate the opposition, particularly Jewish tribes living in Arabia. Two of these tribes were defeated and their goods confiscated; a third tribe, the Benn Koraidha, which surrendered after a seige were massacred to a man. Some seven hundred died, and their property was divided among the conquerors.

War in the name of Islam became jihad, holy war. Each mission was a crusade for which the warriors of Allah would receive a just reward. The Prophet insisted that:

'the sword is the key of heaven; a drop of blood shed in the cause of God, a night spent in arms, avails more than two months of prayer or fasting: he that falls in battle, his sins are all forgiven: at the day of judgement his wounds shall shine as vermillion and smell as musk; angels and cherubin shall give their wings to restore the limbs he has lost.' [6]

The history of Christianity is also tainted—at particular times—with the same kind of mentality. The Crusades against the Islamic Saracens in the Middle Ages, the later depredations of the Spanish in parts of South and Middle America, all tell the same tragic story. And this is not to mention the coercive measures which have been taken by Christians against other Christians to make them conform to a particular doctrinal position or toe a specific ecclesiastical line. The Inquisition instituted by the Catholic Church in the thirteenth century to stamp out heresy is a case in point. It operated throughout most of Western Europe for several centuries, and its activities even spread to the New World. It was particularly zealous in

Spain in its attempts to eliminate not only religious offenders such as Protestants, Jews, Moors (Muslims), mystics and the like, but also moral offenders who might be almost anything from bigamists to homosexuals. Figures are very difficult to compile for this period, but it has been roughly estimated that about three hundred thousand people suffered one way or another at the hands of the Inquisition, which in many ways became a political tool in a religious guise.

World-transforming systems do not always take kindly to opposition and are often bent on rooting out dissident elements when they have the power to do so. Where they lack this power, they may remain or become world-rejecting systems or settle for a mere world-accepting role.

In our own time, this hardly applies any longer to religious movements, as such, but rather to certain quasi-religious political movements and counter-movements which dare not permit the rebellious and the unconvinced to voice their views. Enforced conversion is still often tried, but the really intractable are sometimes not allowed to survive. Some world-transforming systems can be total in their demands.

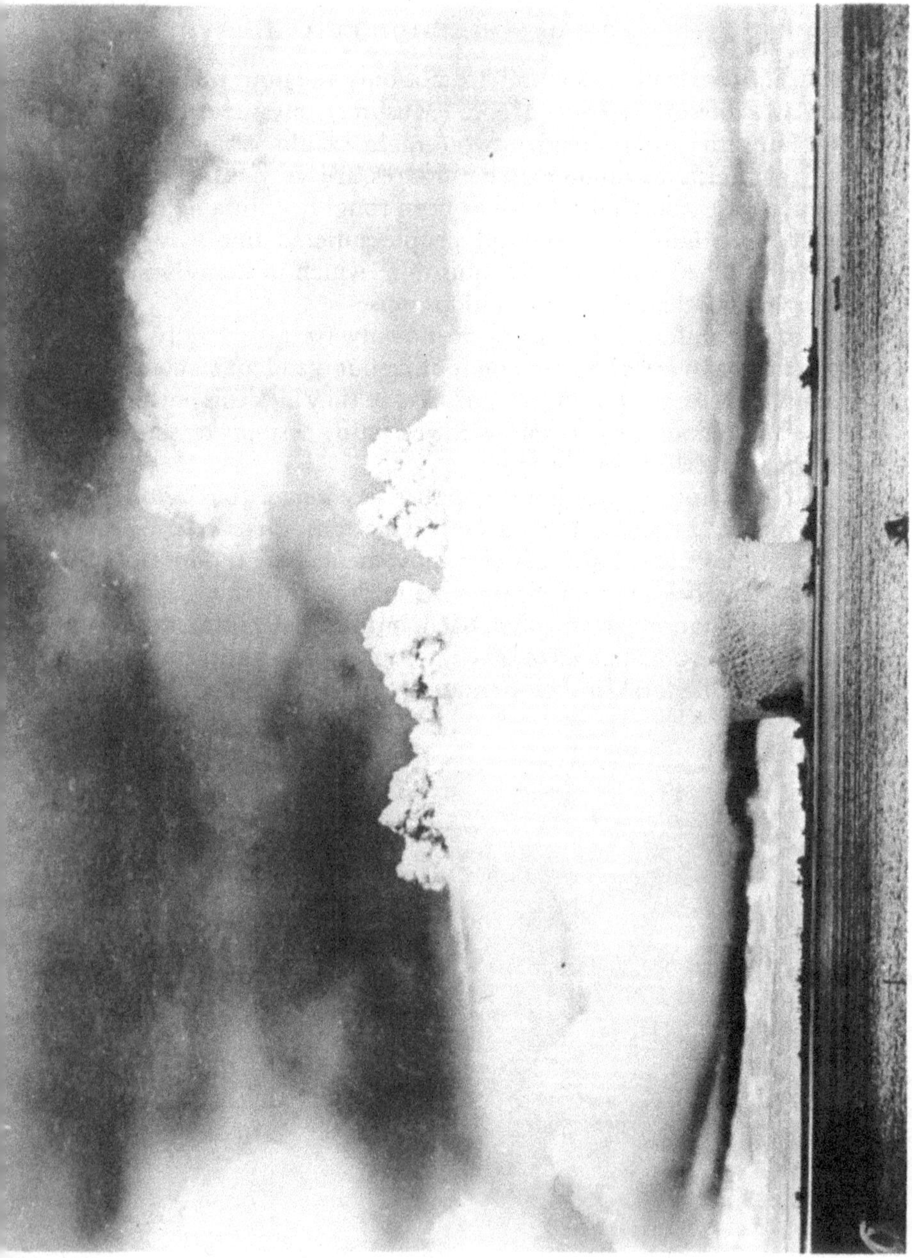

Chapter Five

What purposes does religion serve?

Religion can serve quite specific and distinctive purposes in different societies at different times. The first three hundred years of the history of Christianity was characterized by sporadic and often intensive persecutions by Roman authorities. Particular rulers, Nero, Domitian, Diocletian and others, were intent on stamping out this faith which would not recognize the sovereignty of Rome, and in particular the supreme authority of the Emperor. For those about to be thrown to the lions or butchered by gladiators, religion acted as a source of strength and consolation. It bolstered their courage in the face of certain death, and provided them with an assurance of eternal life which made their agony more bearable—and certainly more meaningful. Centuries later, however, the same religion became the inspiration of a very different cause. The impassioned preaching of Peter the Hermit in the eleventh century AD helped to initiate the series of Christian wars against the Muslims which has been given the rather general—and misleading—title, the Crusades. They were hardly the heroic endeavours of dedicated knights which early histories have depicted. Indeed, the massacres perpetrated against the Muslims, particularly by the one-time schoolboys' idol, Richard I (the Lionheart), during the Third Crusade (AD 1190) showed the Christians to be far less 'Christian'—in the now accepted sense of that term—than their enemies.

In both these instances, we see the *same* religion as both the inspirational idea and supportive mechanism behind two very different movements. Those involved interpreted the same faith in different ways and used it to buttress their arguments, to justify their actions, and gain support for their causes. For the early Christians, the cause was passive resistance to the might of Rome; its effects were slow, but gradually the hostility of the anti-Christian crowds was eroded, and Christianity became an 'accepted' religion—in many ways perhaps the saddest fate of a virile faith. For the Crusaders, the cause was the recapture of the Holy Land, especially Jerusalem, and the slaughter of the infidel Muslims who had desecrated Christian soil; at first the Turks and later the Moors in Spain. To what extent their real motives were religious and to what extent they were political and expansionist, or even acquisitive—because a little plunder on the side was usually welcome—perhaps even *they* were not always sure. What is certain is that religion served as an emotional spur in these campaigns; it was neither the first nor the last time that lofty phrases and noble sentiments about high endeavour have been used to goad men to needless self-sacrifice. The seal of the Church was never lacking to sanctify the questionable zeal of the Crusaders.

But having said all this, was religion really serving very different purposes in each case? In both instances, religion helped to promote solidarity, to band men together in a common cause. It gave them a sense of unity and strength. In addition, it strengthened their resolution, they felt emboldened; it enabled them to face the risks with determination and courage—often heedless of the consequences. Not least of all, it supplied the rationale for their actions, it gave them a sense of the ultimate rightness of their task. Even if the *means* might be in doubt, there was no question about the *goals*. Heaven's reward seemed certain.

So we have arrived at this conclusion, that the purposes religion serves may take different *forms* in different societies at different times, but that basically it functions in much the same way in all societies. This applies as much to primitive as to modern industrialized societies. The main difference concerns the areas of activity within which religion is operative, and this varies from society to society. It would be as well if we now looked more closely at some of these basic functions.

RELIGION AND THE PROBLEM OF MEANING

Professor Elizabeth Nottingham has written,

'Religion is associated with man's attempts to plumb the depths of meaning in both himself and the universe. It has given rise to the most spacious products of his imagination, and it has been used to justify the extremest cruelty of man to man. It can conjure up moods of sublime exaltation, and also images of dread and terror.' [1]

Why are we here? What is life all about? Men have been asking such questions from time immemorial. In the Old Testament Book of Job, an extremely ancient work which takes the form of a play, the character Job questions God because he cannot understand the tragedy of his own situation. 'Where shall wisdom be found? And where is the place of understanding? Man does not know the way to it, and it is not found in the land of the living.' [2]

Science cannot supply the answer. It can advance theories about the origins of life, and guess at the nature of the Universe itself, but these are impersonal speculations, it tells us nothing of the human condition. It can tell us how forces act and how mechanisms function, but these are largely *descriptions*, not explanations in terms of *meaning*. There is little here to satisfy the human spirit. The Universe is still the 'torturer' which, in Ernest Gellner's phrase, 'deprives us of hope, yet does not allow for assured despair' [3].

Although the questions are ageless, every generation is impatient for an answer. In the words of the sociologist, Emile Durkheim, 'Science is fragmentary and incomplete; it advances but slowly and is never finished; but life cannot wait. The theories which are destined to make men live and act are therefore obliged to pass science and complete it prematurely.' [4] It is at this point that religion comes into its own. Total uncertainty is intolerable, we cannot bear not to know. We feel there must *be* a reason, there must be a meaning—if there isn't life becomes 'a tale told by an idiot . . . signifying nothing'. So men have proceeded to *ascribe* a meaning to life, even though they were not always sure how valid this ascription was. In fact, these were very much acts of faith. Religion, among other things, is just that, the meanings which men give to life and the ways in which they explain their existence.

RELIGION AS A MEANS OF CONSOLATION

Walt Whitman had a point when he observed that 'Man is nature's only worrier'. He was suggesting, of course, that only humans have the capacity for reflective thought and that this in turn involves tension and anxiety.

During childhood, most of us are effectively sheltered from those sudden and unpredictable events which appear mainly to overtake adults. With increased maturity and responsibility, we begin to appreciate the nature of these events which are common to all people. Illness, accidents, misfortune, the deaths of friends and relatives, even the prospect of our own death—all these inevitably give us all cause for concern. Fundamentally, they present us with two sets of problems, the first involving once again the question of explanations, the second the additional matter of adjustment.

In simple or pre-scientific societies, people are not ignorant of the laws of cause and effect, but they are not always sure just which cause to connect with which effect. Or they may associate the wrong cause with an effect, as in the case of witchcraft practices. If something calamitous befalls a particular individual and no obvious connection can be established between it and some preceding incident, which is obvious in, say, a serious illness or death resulting from a snakebite, the catastrophe may be ascribed to some other phenomenon with believed ritual associations. For instance, in Polynesia if it can be established that the victim had touched a corpse, or among the Kikuyu of East Africa that the victim had eaten from a cracked pot or had had some contact with a woman's menstrual discharge—and there are many other taboos—this might be taken to account for his condition [5]. Here, religion gives consolation insofar as it provides some kind of answer to the question, 'Why did this happen?' The kind of question that does not appear to be seriously considered in this kind of society is 'Why do such things as corpses, cracked pots, menstrual discharges "contaminate" in this way?' The problem is not really dealt with. It still exists—but at one remove.

At a more 'practical' level, religion provides a means of adjustment to certain situations. At a Christian funeral service, for instance, the 'manifest function' (to use sociological terms) is to honour the dead person and provide a communal occasion whereby relatives and friends can pay him their last respects. It can be argued, however, that the deceased, having now departed, is no longer the real focus of the ceremony. Thus the 'latent function' of the service would be to comfort the bereaved, and to provide a means of adjustment for the living. *They*, not the deceased, must face the full implications of what has happened, and adapt to the new situation resulting from his death. Obviously, the question of an assumed afterlife or otherwise is relevant here, and can be the source of greatest consolation. But this ultimate possibility is beyond the scope of sociology. All that can be said of religion with any assurance is that it provides a set of mechanisms whereby people who necessarily have a great emotional investment in their own lives and in the lives of those dear to them, adjust to the inexorable facts of suffering and death.

RELIGION AS A MEANS OF COMPENSATION

This, of course, is closely allied to the ideas which have been developed in the previous section. As people look around them, they are confronted with inequalities in the distribution of wealth, power and what are usually conceived as the 'means of happiness'. Not only do such inequalities give rise to religious and moral interpretations of the social order insofar as they provoke questions of meaning, they also tend to generate ideas about ultimate justice, an inevitable balancing-of-the-books, either here or in the hereafter. If there is a sense of deprivation *now*, will there be compensation later? 'Truly, I say unto you, there is no man who has left house or wife or brothers or parents or children, for the sake of the Kingdom of God who will not receive manifold more in this time and in the age to come, eternal life' [6]. The suggestion here is that those who are prepared to make the necessary sacrifices will not only be rewarded in this life, but also in the life to come. Does this mean a reward in material terms? This is arguable. Perhaps such promises should be interpreted in less palpable and more spiritual terms, i.e. in the intangible currency of inner contentment.

In a Thornton Wilder novel [7], the would-be evangelist, George Brush, during a momentary lapse, complains that prayer is not for concrete things, but only for abstractions such as guidance and faith, etc. The desire for some kind of compensation for deprivation in this life will not always await postponement until the next, or be content with just non-material rewards. This desire for economic or social justice may take a fairly orthodox 'institutionalized' form, or it may lead to quite extravagant ideas of a 'millennial' type.

Let us examine these possibilities more closely. The most conventional form of compensatory belief may be held by those who make special claims to religious experience. The notion of salvation, whatever may be its spiritual significance, certainly has this function. The convert enjoys a new status which in certain religious communities is celebrated in such a way as to reinforce his conviction that he has now become a member of a select and privileged group. This may be expressed by some rite such as adult baptism by immersion which is practised in some Nonconformist Christian communities.

It has been argued that religious status is particularly attractive to those whose worldly status is insignificant. That those who have menial and unrewarding jobs, or who belong to underprivileged ethnic groups tend to 'transvalue' their work or their otherwise unenviable situations by means of religious reorientation. The spiritual benefits counterbalance the lack of material benefits. This seems to be borne out in this country in relation to the growth of certain kinds of Protestant sects, e.g. the Pentecostals [8], and the high church affiliation figures given for some West Indian immigrants [9]. However, this view must be treated with some reservation for it can be shown [10] that, as a general rule the most economically deprived are those least likely to attend churches. Certainly in the USA and in Britain, it cannot be effectively argued that deprivation leads to increased religious activity, neither can it be maintained that the working classes, presumably the most underprivileged strata, are more religious than others [11].

In more extreme forms, the desire for compensation can lead to millennial expectations. Many religions have 'eschatologies', literally doctrines of the 'last things', which envisage an end to this age or this world order, when the faithful will be rewarded, and the unfaithful punished. The end may be seen as sudden, as Paul puts it 'as a thief in the night' [12], and even cataclysmic. Perspectives vary *within* such religious systems let alone between them. Some think the end may be expected soon, others see it as far distant, but when it comes a new and golden age, the 'millennium', will then be ushered in, and a new world order will begin.

One of the most bizarre examples of this view is to be found among the natives of Melanesia [13]. Their 'Cargo cults' exist where once US service men brought manufactured goods to the islands' inhabitants. The soldiers have long since departed, but the natives, as a ritual, simulate troop movements on the shores in the plaintive hope that the long-awaited 'cargo' will come. They imitate military activities even to the point of wearing mock uniforms and carrying wooden rifles. The belief seems to be that if they repeat the 'white formulae' correctly, the cargo transports cannot fail to appear. For them, the millennium will have arrived when these cargo-laden ships and planes again visit the islands. Only then will the social order be inverted and the natives will wrest authority from the whites and become their own masters once again.

The longing for some kind of redress for the disappointments and frustrations and injustices of this life is a feature of most belief systems. Both religious leaders and philosophers have tried to answer the questions associated with this problem with varying degrees of success. No answer is adequate, but some are persuasive. One of the most plausible is that suggested long ago by Plato, and refined in modern times by the late Professor C. S. Lewis [14]. This is a form of what is technically called the 'ontological argument'. Basically, this advances the seemingly simple idea that if there were no such things as ultimate justice, truth and so on, we should not be aware of them. The very fact that we are deeply conscious of the need of them suggests that somehow they already exist. Of course, it could be argued that men are aware of the idea of unicorns and dragons—but *they* don't exist. But then, it could be countered that unicorns and dragons are not expressions of felt needs. For men's physical and social needs there are known and accessible satisfactions: for hunger there is food; for thirst, drink; for companionship, people; for love there are sexual, parental and filial relationships. In other words, for our subjective needs, there are objective satisfactions. Could this then apply to more abstract longings, which for men are just as 'real' in their own way? When men desire justice, truth, perfection, etc., could it be that for every subjective need there is, perhaps in some afterlife, a corresponding objective satisfaction?

RELIGION AS A SANCTION FOR THE CURRENT SOCIAL ORDER

People not only require a moral explanation for their failures, but also their successes. And it is no modest achievement that men have managed to evolve social arrangements which have resulted in a reasonable degree of harmony. But not only do particular actions need to be justified, the entire social fabric needs to be underpinned by acceptable ethical formulae, and this too can be a function of religion.

Take the example of medieval society. This was highly stratified or 'layered' in terms of classes or, more accurately, 'estates': the land-owning aristocracy, the clergy and the peasants. It was obviously in the interests of the ruling classes that this state of affairs should be perpetuated and the *status quo* maintained. It is not surprising, therefore, that Christian theology tended to support this contention. The serf had little status in socio-economic terms in the feudal order, but it was insisted that his humility was not unnoticed by God. Hell and purgatory were firmly believed in, and seen as the appropriate—indeed, the inevitable—punishments for misconduct in this life. Heaven was the Christian's goal, and all else was, in theory, to be sacrificed to this end. So current religious thinking ascribed moral worth to existing civil society, and even hinted that those of low estate would fare better in the life to come than the aristocracy who for the present were more fortunately placed.

This is not intended to support the proposition that medieval Christian theology was deliberately designed in such a way as to rationalize injustice and promote inequalities. In fact, it is doubtful that medieval man saw the situation in these terms. No doubt some theologians were expressing a bias, and no doubt some members of the ruling classes calculated that this was to their advantage. But, by and large, social arrangements are not—and more often were not—made by deliberate formulations of policy. It is probably more historically accurate to suggest that such policies grew out of the existing social situations. The forms that medieval religion took were products or reflections of the existing social order. The effect was, of course, reciprocal, each influenced the other; the Church in the Middle Ages cannot be divorced from its time.

The interesting, and in some way disturbing, thing about all this is that it doesn't just apply to 'history'. Modern studies of the influence of religion in society show very similar tendencies. In a relatively recent study in the USA, Professor Herberg [15] has shown that the trend in religion there is to

7 Mother and child refugees

minimize the differences between the three major faiths of Protestantism, Catholicism and Judaism. The main contention of this work is the hypothesis that the phenomenon of high church attendance and affiliation figures [16] in the USA can be attributed to the fact that Americans really worship 'Americanism'. Where distinctive religious values do not accord with Americanism, they tend to be discounted. There is an accommodation to worldly values by many religious organizations, and religion has come to reflect the American ideology of a self-improvement society. Religion endorses, so it is claimed, the worldly values of a success and consumption-oriented economy. This is the trend which is designated 'secularization' by the sociologists.

A number of qualifications can be made of this thesis [17], but in very general terms (and not exclusively within the US framework) it provides an interesting and thought-provoking diagnosis of the Western religious scene.

RELIGION AS A REVOLUTIONARY FORCE

Up to this point, we have thought of religion as a reinforcing mechanism which tends to promote unity and enhance social stability. This is not always the case. Religious beliefs can be socially disruptive and lead to radical and even revolutionary movements.

As we shall see (Chapter Seven) there emerge from time to time in many societies, personalities which are roughly classified as religious reformers. Their aim is certainly not to support the *status quo*, but either to generate a spirit of unrest, or to harness the feeling of frustration and discontentment which may already exist. Their intention is rarely the violent overthrow of the existing social order, but usually an attempt to call men back to the fundamental tenets of their religion. In recruiting support for their causes, they may found small sects whose purposes are limited and whose life is short, or they may found movements which change the face of society and even become accepted as new religions.

Once the new movement is given recognition, and its aims accepted, it may find itself spent as a force, and its revolutionary character altered. In the thirteenth century AD both Dominic and Francis, later canonized as saints of the Roman Catholic Church, found the radical nature of their intentions neutralized, and their reforming zeal canalized into the harmless channels of well-intentioned Orders. These did very little to change the essential nature of medieval Catholicism; the same would probably have happened again with Martin Luther, a priest of the Church in the sixteenth century, had Pope Leo X been as astute as his thirteenth-century predecessor. Instead, the Protestant movement developed under Luther and his successors, and challenged the might and waning authority of Catholicism.

On the other hand, the Anabaptist movement in Germany, also in the sixteenth century gave rise to uncompromising and extravagant religious and social practices. It challenged not only the ecclesiastical authority but also the legally constituted governmental authority, and was violently suppressed.

Nearer our own time, a sect of Islam in the Sudan of the last century, led by a prophet known as the Mahdi, followed the example of the seventh-century Muslims who ravaged North Africa and Southern Europe, and translated religious zeal into aggression. It could be argued, with certain very important reservations, that their modern counterparts are those of the Black Muslim movement, now enjoying such a vogue in the USA, who likewise advocate the violent overthrow of 'order', i.e. white American authority. All in the name of religion.

It can hardly be maintained, as certain Marxist or near-Marxist writers have done, that most—if not all—religious movements are really pre-political. This view holds that because men, often in underprivileged circumstances, cannot find political expression, their movements take on a religious character. Religion, according to this theory, is really only a substitute for political action. However, not all religions are religions of protest, some indeed are religions of *renunciation*, e.g. Hinduism and Buddhism. Where religion takes a violent form, this may be determined not so much by its own internal ethic, as by the nature of the opposition which it encounters and the social forces prevailing at the time [18]. In general, religion can be seen, in social terms as the varying response to men's relatively unvarying needs.

8 'Telephone book cure' in Kenya

Chapter Six

How does religion function in different societies?

The discussion in this chapter is really an extension of two theoretical points which were made in Chapter Five. Here we will examine the social characteristics and the social role of religion in actual contexts. Some comparisons will be made between different types of society and particular emphasis will be given to the differing functions of religion in pre-industrial as opposed to industrial societies. This division can be roughly equated with the distinction which sociologists make between undifferentiated and differentiated societies.

As far as religion is concerned, an undifferentiated society is one where the institutional role of religion cannot be clearly distinguished from other aspects of the social complex. Thus in pre-industrial societies religion 'merges' with the economic, domestic, political and educational institutions of those societies—insofar as these too can be distinguished. Its influence permeates the entire fabric of these societies in such a way that it may not be seen as a clear and separate area of concern. For example, the laws in pre-industrial societies are often of a religious or semi-religious character, and even the apparently non-religious aspects of their codes may well be upheld by religious sanctions. This is particularly so where, as in the Trobriand Islands, the chief is believed to be able to invoke supernatural powers as an aid in maintaining social control.

By contrast, a differentiated society, therefore, is a society much like our own. It is a society in which scientific and commercial advances have brought about a high degree of specialization. The modern world deals in larger units than simple societies, and this in turn has led to a compartmentalization of concern which, in general, has not favoured religious interests. Beliefs and practices which once had a pervasive influence in society have now been largely relegated to smaller —and perhaps more ineffectual—areas of personal concern. This is a theme which we will take up again towards the end of the chapter.

To begin then with undifferentiated societies, we must look at those communities where it is possible to see:

RELIGION AS THE SOURCE OF ULTIMATE EXPLANATION

It should be made clear at the outset that this does not mean that religion is viewed as the source of *total* explanation, it is doubtful whether this state of affairs has ever existed anywhere. In all societies, men have been prepared to manipulate religion to their own advantage, and it has never provided an absolute code which governed their total experience. On the other hand, it is not difficult to find societies where religion has provided the *ultimate* source of explanation. There are large 'gaps' in the knowledge of every society even those possessed of advanced scientific techniques, consequently there are numerous questions which still go unanswered. There is an assumption that eventually science will provide those answers and put an end to theological speculation. In pre-scientific societies, these areas of the unknown are obviously very extensive, by our standards, but in this case they are 'filled' by non-naturalistic explanations. Thus, to cite the Trobrianders once again, when asked why certain parts of the islands are sacred, they will refer to respected mythical traditions which assert that these are where their ancestors 'first saw the sun'.

Religion, therefore, is integral to the 'world-view' of such societies. It helps to structure the thinking of their members about the nature of the world and of their place in the general scheme of things. These 'views' may not be commonly held even by members of the same society. Anthropologists often find considerable variations in the beliefs of a single community —but this is also true of advanced societies which exhibit all manner of inconsistencies especially in matters of religious belief. There is always a marked disparity between what is supposed to be believed and what is actually believed, and an even greater disparity between beliefs and practices. It is for this reason that investigators tend to concentrate upon what people do rather than what they say (although, it must be admitted, they often have to accept what people *say they do*).

In non-literate societies, there can be no codified beliefs. Values are transmitted symbolically in rituals, as they still are in our own society—though to a much lesser extent. Ritual acts are the 'language' of belief. On specific and regular occasions, they 'announce' the values which are commonly held concerning such things as birth, maturity, marriage, fertility, war and death. Perhaps the clearest idea of what any society believes can be gained from an examination of its rituals—but even this does not obviate the problem of the interpretation of these rituals. It is, in fact, something of a 'chicken-and-egg' question as to whether ritual precedes belief or whether belief precedes ritual. It is probably still the more popular 'common-sense' view that beliefs give rise to ritual practices, but the view of many anthropologists is that beliefs are really intellectualizations of ritual acts, attempts to make rational sense of what has been done in that society since time immemorial.

These points about religion and explanation can best be illustrated by a glance at two actual belief systems in simple societies. The first is a pervasive, widely distributed set of phenomena which are usually grouped together under the general title of witchcraft, and the second is a specific set of beliefs and practices found among the Lovedu of the Transvaal.

(a) *Witchcraft: a Closed System of Explanation*

Witchcraft beliefs take very many forms, and are to be found in various societies in all ages, although they are particularly prevalent in many—but by no means all—primitive societies. In fact, it is possible to find neighbouring societies, one of which has such beliefs and another which has not; the Mesakin and the Korongo in the Sudan are a case in point [1].

Essentially, witch beliefs can be reduced to the fact that some people put the blame for some of their sufferings on a peculiar power which is usually regarded as evil. This power is either seen as something which can be manipulated or served by individuals, or—more commonly in primitive societies—as something which is embodied in certain individuals, 'although no material connection can be empirically demonstrated between those individuals and the ills they are supposed to have caused' [2]. In the former instance, which is characteristic of witchcraft in medieval Europe, where the evil power is associated with the Devil, witchcraft beliefs have a supernatural content, and may therefore be rightly regarded as forms of religion. In the latter case, where the power is believed to reside in the individuals, it is debatable whether it can be considered religious at all, although the beliefs certainly contain a non-natural if not a supernatural element.

Uncanny powers are attributed to witches. They may be thought to be able to fly or to change their form at will; the American Navaho Indians, for example, believed they took a werewolf form. Witches are almost invariably thought to be adults, and these may often be recognized by certain physical peculiarities such as the 'devil's mark'. This might be a mere birth mark, but if it was found, especially on the breasts or the genitalia (a sure sign of collusion with the Devil!), it could warrant torture and even death in sixteenth-century Europe.

A particularly interesting form of witch belief which has been well documented [3], is to be found among the Azande peoples of Africa. The Azande belief that a person is a witch by virtue of a mysterious witchcraft substance or mangu in the body. This inherited capacity for witchcraft may be dormant in any person, and may well be exercised unconsciously. As Professor Evans-Pritchard puts it 'A witch performs no rite, utters no spell, and possesses no medicines. An act of witchcraft is a psychic act. . . .' Ill-will and resentment are believed to cause the witchcraft substance to be active—the Zande talk about being 'hot'.

In practice, a witchcraft 'case' begins with a calamity or mishap of some kind. A near relative of the 'victim' will then make a witchcraft accusation against the person who is supposed to be exercising the evil powers. Not surprisingly, this may be another near relative or someone who is too powerful or senior to be 'reached' in any other way. Some kind of divination will probably follow by recognized practitioners, sometimes referred to as witchdoctors. This may take the form of test which may well be weighted against the accused; the Zande, for instance, employ a 'poison oracle' system. If the guilt of the accused is 'established' they may be allowed to make restitution, or they will be punished in the prescribed way. This could be horrible in the extreme in particular societies. In a primitive society such as the Zulu in the early part of the last century, the 'witch'—particularly if he was thought to have been practising against the royal person—was pinioned by the King's executioners, and wooden rods were hammered into his anus until he died. At the same time warriors were dispatched to destroy his huts and his family, and to destroy or confiscate his goods. On the other hand, in a so-called civilized society, Western Europe in the sixteenth century, witches were usually burned with the added refinement of preliminary torture.

To those who accept it, witchcraft can be a closed intellectual system. Often they are aware of the natural order of things, but are unaware of the extent of that natural order. What matters is the *context* in which events occur. *Why* do they happen? And why do they happen to *that* person, and why do they happen *then*? So witchcraft becomes the answer for everything that cannot be otherwise explained. It has the function of releasing social tensions and suppressed animosities. In its own way, it 'accounts' for the evils in society—especially in its rather sophisticated Zande evil-from-within form. No satisfactory evidence has ever been forthcoming to show that there is any *causal* connection between the practices of witches and the fortunes or misfortunes of their intended victims. The consequences of 'detection' have been frightening, but as a theory of experience, witchcraft is certainly no worse than attributing the inexplicable to 'chance'.

A very different system of explanation is associated with ancestor worship, although witchcraft beliefs and beliefs in ancestral spirits are by no means mutually exclusive. Certainly in many African societies they exist together, but have somewhat different functions.

(b) *Ancestor Cults: a Reflective System of Explanation*

Ancestor worship or veneration is another set of beliefs with a very wide distribution. It provides a kind of structured support for a society insofar as worship of the ancestors is really an extension of the authority structure which normally exists in that society. This can best be judged by seeing how it works among a particular people, the Lovedu of the Transvaal.

The Lovedu are atypical inasmuch as they are ruled by a woman, the Rain-Queen. Traditionally, the Lovedu themselves comprised a tribal élite which controlled a number of other heterogeneous tribal groups. The authority of the Rain-Queen is mediated through senior lineage-heads down to the leaders of small kin-groups who act as local headmen. Tribute is paid to the Queen in the form of daughters who are 'redistributed' as wives among the lineage-heads. This serves to cement the bonds between the Queen and her chiefs, and increase their sense of loyalty and obligation.

The Lovedu assume that nature can be controlled by the use of powers concentrated in certain persons, primarily the Rain-Queen herself and some specialist 'doctors' who are thought to be possessed or guided by ancestor spirits. The Queen is believed to be so 'bound up' with nature that even her emotions affect the rain, and her death is thought to dislocate the natural order.

The ancestors are propitiated by offerings and prayer. This is carried on at all levels of the society from the family upwards, and customarily involves senior males, although women also play some part in these ritual activities. The ancestors are regarded as capricious and unpredictable in their actions. However, they can only influence—for good or ill—the fortunes of their *own* descendants. The exception is, of course, the Queen's ancestors who can affect the entire tribe. The degree of neglect or veneration seems to bear little relation to the amount of satisfaction received, but when protection is not given and, say, a man dies, it may be excused on the grounds that the ancestors have 'had an accident'.

The ancestors have only a place—although a well-appointed place—in a pantheon of other more mystical spirits. Witchcraft and sorcery seem to occupy an even more prominent position in the Lovedu mind, and more misfortunes are attributed to them than to the ancestors. What is not clear is just how the source of any particular misfortune is to be determined [4]. Although the 'doctors' and the oracles always help in this respect.

The main functions of the Lovedu ancestor worship would seem to be in the ways it serves to maintain the existing social structure. The cult of the ancestors—as distinct from other kinds of ritual practices—could be seen as a logical extension of the reverence for age found in so many primitive societies. It is a system calculated to buttress respect for the aged in subsistence societies where a premium is usually put upon prowess and virility, and where a survivalist-type ethic might prevail and the weak and the old might 'go to the wall'.

Further, there is an obvious ranking of the ancestral spirits and this reflects the authority structure which already exists in the society itself. Therefore, if the tribal gods and 'cosmic forces' are not accessible to the people, as appears to be the case, the people can only secure highly prized benefits, such as rain, by continued loyalty and tribute—usually through district heads—to the Queen who alone is thought able to obtain those benefits.

Belief in the equal accessibility of the god or gods tends to render 'divine' and ritual heads unnecessary. It may be that there is some correlation between the Protestant principle of 'the priesthood of all believers' and the democratic ideal.

RELIGION AS A SYSTEM OF SELECTIVE EXPLANATION

In more complex pre-industrial societies, religion becomes institutionalized. This means that there are usually cultic centres with highly elaborate rituals, a hierarchy of paid priests who administer these centres, and codified regulations governing the worship procedures. Beliefs and practices are harmonized into coherent systems which are then perpetuated as part of a tradition.

It should be made clear, however, that in particular societies of this kind, religion has been a source of ultimate explanation. This would certainly be true of the Aztecs of Mexico in the late fifteenth century (see Volume I), and a number of other societies at particular times. But, in general, where religion is only one very highly esteemed part of a society which has become increasingly differentiated with the development of complex institutions, one detects that it functions as a political and economic aid rather than an integral support. It must be stressed that this would have to be considerably qualified in special cases, but, in the main, political and economic considerations appear to predominate in this type of society, with religion providing the necessary supportive sanctions.

Some systems have been very flexible in this respect, and others have been notoriously inflexible. Perhaps we should look at some examples of both types in turn.

(a) *The Flexible System: Ancient Greece*

The term 'ancient Greece' is, in itself, a little vague. For our purposes, it denotes the 'golden Age' period which lasted approximately from 500 to 400 BC.

The Greeks worshipped a pantheon of gods led by Zeus, the Father of the Gods. But even the term worship should be qualified. The gods, associated traditionally with Mount Olympus, were little more than men 'writ large'. They seem to have been subject to the same passions and weaknesses as ordinary mortals, but without human justifications. Admittedly, they were believed to be possessed of certain magical powers, but even these they employed arbitrarily. The pre-golden Age writers such as Homer and Hesiod, who apparently accepted them, emphasize their capriciousness. Later writers, particularly the philosophers and some of the dramatists, seem to have adopted a much more sceptical attitude. In general, then, it might be more accurate to say that the Greeks acknowledged the gods in greater or lesser degrees.

There is some evidence, as seen in Chapter Three, that many Greeks were still attached to the very primitive 'cults of the hearth', the many 'earth' deities which were worshipped on a household basis. These almost certainly had associations with fertility, and possibly there were connections with the fertility religions which were common throughout the Near and Middle East, and which date from the pre-history period.

The Greek temples were not worship centres in our sense of the term. Architectural masterpieces such as the Parthenon in Athens which cost about half the annual income of the state (i.e. the Athenian polis) when it was built in the fifth century BC, really existed to house the gods—or, at least, their images. There was no paid clergy, as we understand the term, although some priests did officiate at special centres such as Delphi. This centre had a very versatile magico-economic role, the Oracle could be consulted there, but it was also available as a banking-house, and huge treasures were sometimes deposited with the priests.

Greek religion was not really geared to the needs of the various states either for educational or political purposes. It acted very much as an occasionally influential addition. There were times when religion appears to have played a crucial part in state affairs, for example, during the Persian wars which went on intermittently in one form or another throughout the century. But even here, as with the condemnation of Socrates in 399 BC on a charge of blasphemy, it is difficult to escape the suspicion that religion was being used for political ends. The relatively peripheral place of religion in Ancient Greece becomes even more evident when we compare its role with that of religion in, say, medieval England. Both were politically decentralized, but in Greece, religion was also decentralized, whereas the medieval Church was a highly centralized, almost monolithic, system. Contrasted with Christianity in the Middle Ages, Greek religion was a rather light-weight affair. It was, in general, a system which was both accommodating and adaptable, centred theologically on a pantheon of colourful deities whom people found it increasingly difficult to take seriously.

(b) *The Inflexible System: Ancient Sumeria*

The gods of Sumeria or Southern Mesopotamia (modern Iraq) were worshipped in one form or another for over three thousand years. More is probably known about the successive civilizations of ancient Iraq than those in any other part of the world. Thousands of tablets have been unearthed, particularly in the remains of the Assyrian city of Nineveh; the translations of many of these have not yet been published. For the purposes of this brief discussion, we will take the typical conditions of the period 2700 to 2000 BC.

It may be that in no other ancient society did religion occupy such a prominent position, 'because in no other antique society did man feel himself so utterly dependent on the will of the gods' [5]. Sumeria was divided politically into a number of city-states which consisted of the cities proper together with their surrounding villages, orchards, palm-groves and fields. Each city and its territory were owned by the god who acted as its 'protector'. The people too belonged to the local deity, and so, by definition, did the fruits of their labours. Some of the free citizens had titular ownership of lands, but the nominal ownership was that of the deity for whom the people were theoretically stewards. It is still a matter of debate whether the lands were really regarded as the property of the gods or of the nobility who comprised a religious caste. In all probability, they belonged to the gods, in theory, but in practice they effectively belonged to those who administered and derived their incomes from them.

This can be seen from the way in which the system actually operated. The temples possessed their own fields and pastures which were cultivated exclusively for those who served them. The remainder of the cultivated land was divided into three parts. One part was 'the land of the Lord' and was worked by the entire community for the benefit of the temple. A second part was allotted to the dependents of the temple, and a third part was let out to tenants at a rent of one-seventh or one-eighth of the harvest.

It can be seen from this that temple estates and concerns were very big business. The temples disposed of huge revenues; their priests were involved in the tasks of storage and redistribution, and they carried on a great deal of secondary trade, particularly outside Sumeria. The entire population was, in effect, at their disposal for all manner of public works which, at certain periods, were very ambitious in this 'advanced' ancient society. The state was run by a well-organized clerical bureaucracy which, in turn, controlled a vast army of inspectors, overseers and other officials. All were responsible to the clergy who regulated the economy, and ultimately to the ruler of the state who was the chief priest. The king combined the functions of army leader, chief justice, head of the clergy and minister of public works.

As in Greece, enormous sums were expended on public works; cities were beautified at the cost of the private sector of the economy. In Sumeria, this mainly concerned the building and the restoration of temples which one authority, Georges Roux, sees as the 'consequence of the belief that humanity had been created for the service of the gods, and that the ruler was the first of their servants'.

Such a 'commission' gave almost unlimited authority to the ruler. For when political power is buttressed by supernatural sanctions, the ruler can virtually command unquestioning obedience. In some systems, however, this authority has been vested in the office rather than the person. This has meant that the mandate could be transferred—even by *coup d'état*—from one ruler to another in the belief that it is not the man that matters, but the position he holds.

In the Sumerian city-state of Ur, at a particular period in its history, we have a classic example of the importance of this authority. When the king died, the entire royal household was also put to death. At Ur, the king was buried together with his wife, musicians, court ladies, soldiers and numerous servants. The remains indicate that they were first drugged and then killed, and there is the suggestion that this may have been a voluntary act. This practice was not exclusive to Sumeria, but it has been highlighted there by the dramatic discovery of this particular Royal Cemetery by the archeologist, Sir Leonard Woolley [6].

Even in this notably theocentric (god-centred) society, the non-religious functions of religion are obvious. In all probability, the members of the society did not differentiate between religious and non-religious, as we tend to do. There is little doubt that everyone, including the rulers, regarded themselves as mere servants of the gods. Therefore everything that was done affected the gods and their welfare; every act either pleased or displeased them. Retrospectively, however, we can see that whatever was believed about the theocratic (god-ruled) nature of this society, it was in practice positively autocratic, and religion was used, consciously or otherwise, to justify the unchanging order of things. There is no evidence to suggest that it was a *contrived* politico-economic tool, but the effect was much the same for those concerned.

This can be seen especially in the justifications for war. In the much later Assyrian period (911–612 BC), it was believed that the divine hierarchy of gods had their counterparts on earth, thus their representative, the king of Assyria, had to show that his god, Ashur, was supreme by defeating the followers of other gods. Terrorism and massacre on an incalculable scale were religiously justifiable on the grounds that the king's enemies were also the god's enemies. Assyrian monarchs recorded their campaigns with pride. For example, Ashurnasirpal II (d. 859 BC), recalls, 'To the city of Suru . . . I drew near, and the terror of the splendour of Ashur, my lord, overwhelmed them . . . In the valour of my heart and the fury of my weapons, I stormed the city. All the rebels they seized and delivered them up. . . .' Those who rebelled against the king and refused him tribute insulted the gods and usually paid an awful price. The massacres are detailed and recounted in a self-satisfying way, '. . . I flayed all the chiefs who had revolted and covered the pillar with their skin . . . some I walled up . . . some I impaled . . . on stakes. Many captives from among them I burned with fire . . . From some I cut off their noses, their ears and their fingers, of many I put out their eyes. I made one pillar of the living and another of heads. Their young men and maidens I burned. . . .' and so on. The conclusion is unavoidable that whatever autocrats of this kind *believed* they were doing, the 'rightness' of their cause was conveniently justified in terms of religion. By conscious or, in a qualified sense, unconscious manipulation, the will of the gods was made consonant with the ambitions of their servants. Religion has been made mutely answerable for the grossest excesses. But human responsibility cannot easily be displaced.

RELIGION AS A MEANS OF MARGINAL EXPLANATION

In our kind of society, i.e. an advanced, scientifically oriented society, it is maintained that religion no longer has a structurally supportive function, and is hardly a politico-economic aid—though this might have to be seriously qualified in some societies especially where Roman Catholicism is still a force to be reckoned with. Instead, in our predominantly secular society, it is argued that religion is little more than a moral influence [7].

The problem of the decline of religion has already been traced and discussed (Volume 1, Chapter Six). What is required here is some examination of religion as a system of explanation. In this respect, there is little doubt that it has been relegated to the margins of the modern mind. People no longer tend to think in its terms or within its framework. This is not to say that there is a decline in some religious beliefs even if there is a marked decline in many religious practices. This is still a matter of debate, and is the subject of some recent investigations [8]. What *is* being said is that traditional religious values no longer really inform people's actions and aspirations, except perhaps in a rather diffuse kind of way. These changes, together with the resultant accommodation process which has taken place within institutionalized religion is usually summed up in the term secularization. This, according to one authority, is 'the process whereby religious thinking, practice and institutions lose [their] social significance' [9], and has been reasonably well documented in this country and particularly in the United States [10].

The argument is that rationality has now supplanted religion, and that rationality implies acceptance of a scientifically oriented cause-and-effect world. There is no longer any need of recourse to the gods, man's ingenuity can provide—either actually or potentially—all the necessary explanations. Meanwhile, it is conceded that there are one or two vexing questions which still remain unanswered, such as the meaning of existence and the problem of death. But these are thought to be of little *practical* importance. Such questions are held to be expressions of man's emotionality rather than his rationality, and therefore permit of 'temporary' religious explanations which are peripheral to the real business of living.

The notion of rationality is associated with the problem of means and ends. Rational action is said to be action which is calculated to achieve given or chosen ends. On this definition, religious action seems at best non-rational if not positively irrational. This is particularly so with regards to prayer.

Take a simple but actual case. A few years ago, a Pentecostal community wanted a new church, and therefore had to decide how this was to be done. They were not particularly prosperous people, so the task was not easy. Given the nature of the end to be achieved, the means would seem to be obvious, the securing of a long-term loan or mortgage. The Pentecostals, however, decided instead on a series of prayer-meetings. They felt, not unnaturally, that they did not want to make demands of 'outsiders' who were not particularly sympathetic to their cause. At the same time, they were great believers in the old evangelical dictum that if men attempt great things for God, they have every right to expect great things from God. To the impartial observer, their actions make no rational sense. But the fervour which was generated at the prayer meetings so strengthened their resolve that they sold personal possessions, mortgaged their *own* homes and gave the money to the cause. Eventually, having raised just a few thousand pounds, they obtained the services of a believing master-builder, and all laboured together to build their own church. In a sense, therefore, it could be argued that prayer 'worked'. Whether this should be interpreted in an objective sense, is open to dispute, but certainly in a psycho-social sense its goals could be said to have been realized. In this case, non-rationality made its own peculiar kind of sense. But naturally, this instrumental use of prayer could hardly be guaranteed to work in every situation. In general, prayer and other religious practices tend only to operate 'effectively' in extreme and marginal situations.

Further, with regards to this whole business of explanation, it can be seriously doubted whether the attitudes of people towards religion are really changing. Marx, for example, argued that historically people had been in the thrall of religion. He maintained that it had influenced their actions and dominated their thinking in a way which constituted a 'false consciousness', a misapprehension of their own situation. Marx had some very interesting and pertinent things to say about the 'alien' character of the state, about capital and the nature of values and class, etc., but in applying the same general analysis to religion, he seems to have been on rather more uncertain ground. It is arguable whether people have ever, except in certain particular instances, been completely at the mercy of religious belief. The study of religion suggests the contrary, namely that other considerations, especially politico-economic ones have dominated men's thinking in all ages and in all societies.

In functionalist terms, it can be argued that men have almost invariably evolved the forms of religion which provided economic and psycho-social supports. Furthermore, in the observance of such systems, men have always tended to be eclectic in that they have chosen to recognize and obey those things which suited them. This was probably never more so than in our own scientifically advanced societies where religious institutions are ignored and religious imperatives are largely discounted. In this humanistic environment, religion survives residually in *privatized* rather than institutionalized forms. Outward expressions and organized rituals are on the wane, and religion remains as a marginal moral support, an uncertain hope—a personal faith.

Chapter Seven

Is there such a thing as revelation?

Religious movements have their foundations in real or assumed 'revelations'. On a sociological analysis, they may seem to come into being for socio-economic reasons, but the movement itself will almost invariably justify its existence in apocalyptic terms. The word apocalyptic literally means to 'take from cover', to reveal, and movements see their existence as the natural outcome of special insights which have been supernaturally given. This revelation can take many forms, but, in general, it is believed that it is given either to:

(a) The founder of the movement, who may claim to be a prophet or even a messiah. He will certainly lay claim to special insights which he has either gained from experience, as in the case of Gautama the Buddha (the 'enlightened one'), or which have been revealed supernaturally, as with the Old Testament prophets. This attracts followers who are encouraged to share these insights which derive from the founder.

(b) Each individual follower or believer has a particular revelation which has common or shared elements. So Buddhists are enjoined to become 'enlightened' and share the experience of their founder, and would-be Christians are required to seek a conversion experience which will unite them by faith to Christ.

So despite the fact that to sociologists, religion can only be studied as a social phenomenon, it remains for countless people something which has a validity for quite other reasons. For them, it is a revealed faith. It is important, therefore, to try to analyse the phenomena of 'revealed faiths', to discover the forms they take, and to try to isolate their salient features. Having done this, we should be in a better position to judge the validity or otherwise of their claims.

THE MEDIATION OF REVELATION

Despite the great diversity of experiences, revelations fall into a few well-attested categories. The recipients of these mystical insights usually claim that they have either *discovered*—which strictly speaking cannot be classed as revelation except in a carefully qualified sense—or *been given* a new understanding or 'truth'. This truth may be purely personal for them only, or it may be regarded as something which has to be proclaimed or shared with others.

Revelation can be mediated in a number of ways. It may, for instance, be seen as:

(i) *A Reward for Contemplation*

This links, to some extent, with the notion which we have already considered, that mystical experiences can be artificially induced. These attempts to 'secure' such experiences can be seen in a wider spectrum of religious traditions. The extravagances of certain practitioners of Yoga [1], for example, can be compared with the fastings and scourgings of Roman Catholic mystics.

On the other hand, there are recorded instances of how counter-productive such practices can be. Martin Luther insisted that all his fastings and prostrations were of no avail. He stressed the pointlessness of self-torture, and argued that the 'truth' can come simply and unexpectedly. In this case, the 'truth' that indirectly helped to spearhead the Protestant Reformation. This kind of experience compares with that of, say, Gautama who, according to one tradition, after years of fruitless searching, found the key to happiness in the abolition of desire. He had been obsessed with the universal fact of decay and longed to discover that which was imperishable.

'Perfect knowledge' is said to have been revealed to him, after all his intellectual and physical exertions, as he rested under a Bodhi tree.

Perhaps, in these cases, the attempts to experience a revelation were indirectly productive rather than counter-productive. The psychological preconditions as well as the spiritual endeavour were obviously already present. Although the actual insights apparently came as the unintended consequences of religious self-denial.

(ii) *A Means of or as the Result of a Traumatic Experience*

This would include the traditional ways in which revelations are said to be mediated; by trances, dreams and visions.

Within the Judeo-Christian tradition, such experiences are seen to mark, if not to explain, certain radical transformations in particular individuals. The well-known Burning Bush story about Moses would be a case in point. This rather misty but almost certainly authentic figure emerged from relative obscurity to become the Israelites' national leader. Similarly, there is the case of Saul of Tarsus. This man, who was probably a member of the Sanhedrin, the governing Jewish Council, was bent on the eradication of the new and heretical movement which afterwards came to be known as Christianity. He admits that he 'approved of the death of Stephen' (Acts 22: 20), traditionally the first of the Christian martyrs, after which he 'made havoc of the church by entering one house after another, dragging off men and women to prison' (Acts 8: 1–3). Subsequently, he claims to have been confronted with a vision of Christ on the Damascus road which changed his whole way of life. He became Paul, certainly the greatest of the early apostles of Christianity. So here we find someone who helped both to instigate and operate a policy of violent persecution, suddenly becoming the most zealous advocate of the faith he had previously condemned. Later writers have suggested that Paul was seized by remorse or had suffered an epileptic fit or a bout of sunstroke (he was blind after the 'experience' for several days), but this all seems rather facile in view of the radical nature of the transformation which he underwent. Whatever happened—and he insisted that *he knew* what it was—it brought about the conversion of an avowed opponent who became the new faith's most notable apologist.

The question of what happened to change the original disciples from a band of extremely frightened men to the effective co-founders of the Christian Church, falls into the same category. They too claimed to have had an experience of the supernatural. Like Paul, they insisted that they had seen a resurrected Christ. Again, whatever other interpretations can be put upon these incidents something quite traumatic occurred to transform their entire lives. It is still worth noting that their convictions led the majority of them to some form of martyrdom.

Attempts have been made to explain such phenomena naturalistically, but none of these is wholly satisfactory. The experiences were quite devastating to those concerned, and it is doubtful whether what we are able to offer are anything other than descriptions of these events; *explanations* can never be any more than tentative hypotheses. Even to 'explain' a thing—in qualified terms—is not necessarily to explain it *away*. It may always retain an element of mystery which is beyond the scope of scientific enquiry.

THE CHANNEL OF REVELATION

Where a revelation is held to constitute the basis of a religious movement, it is usually believed to be primarily the experience of the founder which is then shared with a faithful nucleus of followers. Founders of movements often defy adequate analysis. Students of religion tend to differentiate between prophets and messiahs, teachers and reformers and mystics [2]. But in fact, founders may combine many if not all of these functions. They may also be regarded as social agitators, charlatans, and even gods.

The 'quality' that is most frequently associated with them in sociological literature is that of 'charisma'. This term, popularized by Max Weber [3], really denotes someone who has the power to command loyalty and devotion from others. As Weber puts it, charisma is 'a certain quality of an individual personality by virtue of which he is set apart from ordinary men and treated as endowed with supernatural, superhuman or at least specifically exceptional powers . . . on [this] basis . . . the individual is treated as a leader'. This idea is really rather interesting, and therefore needs more elaboration and perhaps more critical analysis.

For Weber, charisma was a spontaneous quality. It was not easy to determine its cause or its operation either in particular individuals or in particular situations. To this extent, it was unstable and unharnessed, and therefore likely to be a source of change and innovation. To this extent, it lends support to the unfashionable 'great man' theory of history which holds that although certain leaders are thrown up, as it were, by the circumstances of their time, they also take command of situations and make their own distinctive impressions upon the course of events.

Charisma is also very out-of-the-ordinary, it is 'marked', it is something to be noted. In short, it has a 'presence' which commands attention and which inspires admiration in others. This has certainly been the case with many religious leaders. The Gospel writers sometimes speak of the 'look' of Jesus, and the occasions when no one 'dare question him'. Similarly, participants in the trials of Nazi war-criminals at Nuremburg, testify that some of the defendants could be seen to be visibly moved by the showing of the old films of Hitler speaking at earlier Nuremburg rallies; the dead Fuehrer was still able to cast the charismatic spell. The difficulty with this idea of 'presence' becomes evident, however, when anyone tries to press the association between charisma and the recipients of purported revelations. These have sometimes had anything but 'presence', in the commonly understood sense of the word. There are instances where revelations have been claimed by the ignorant and the uneducated: Mary the mother of Jesus, Joan of Arc and Bernadette of Lourdes would fall into this category. Sometimes they have been people who were very well-meaning but not very bright, such as the original apostles whom Jesus often upbraided for their lack of perception. On the other hand, there were those who were educated but unattractively coarse like Martin Luther, or knowledgeable but bumptious like John Wesley the founder of Methodism. Indeed, at the 'lower end' of the scale, there are those who on any impartial judgement might be considered cases for treatment, such as Saint Simon Stylites who spent his latter days up on a pillar, or the epileptic shamen of certain Asiatic tribes. This is not to invalidate the religious experiences of such people; to try to do so would put us in the pontifical position of deciding who should have revelations and who should not. This is something we are quite unable to do. But it does indicate that at least some claimed revelations are just a little unlikely—not to say implausible.

The last thing we should note about charisma is that it is creative, and in this sense is morally neutral. It can be a characteristic, as we have already observed, of a Jesus or a Hitler. It can be exhibited by a butcher of men such as Timur the Tartar who left pyramids of skulls in his conquered territories, or a non-violent 'prophet' such as Mahatma Gandhi. Charisma is manifest in the evil and the good—however we care to interpret those terms. It is, therefore, quite impossible to lay down rules for revelation. Only in the most general terms, can we characterize the recipients of claimed experiences of this kind. As we have seen, the whole notion of charisma only describes one set of known variables, it explains virtually nothing.

One final theoretical point in this section of the discussion. An important qualification should be made of vision or revelation-based systems. Where visions or 'messages' become an accepted form of revelation, the system is always susceptible to the possibility of further and perhaps divisive revelations. More visions by ambitious subordinates or followers can lead to fragmentation and schism. The 'heretical' movements within Christianity are a case in point. The Mormons and the

Jehovah's Witnesses are just two well-known examples of this phenomenon; in both instances there is an acceptance of the basic tenets of the Judeo-Christian tradition, but with the additions of further special revelations to the founders of those movements. The special revelations or additional features comprise the 'differentiae' of these movements.

THE MAIN CHARACTERISTICS OF REVEALED RELIGIONS

The discussion in this section must be very general because there are many exceptions to the rule. Innumerable questions are begged by the whole idea of revelation, and as far as revelation as a basis for religious movements is concerned, so much hinges on the problem of the nature of the revelation. However, for general purposes, we can delineate the *main* characteristics as follows:

(i) *Revealed Religions are often 'High' Religions*

This idea of revelation plays a large part in those highly developed, world religious systems which have a mass following, a marked ethical content, and well-established traditions. But these 'high' religions, although they have certain things in common—particularly their ethical teaching—must be redefined to point up their differences. Religious systems can be analysed in many ways (as we noted in Chapter Four), but for the purposes of this particular discussion, they can be differentiated as:

(a) *Monotheistic Systems*. These are based on the worship of *one* God only. Judaism, Christianity and Islam are the obvious examples.

(b) *Polytheistic Systems*. Here there is the worship of *many* gods who may represent different areas, different political or family 'groups' or simply different needs or aspects of experience. Hinduism would be the prime example, plus countless other tribal religions. A refinement of polytheism which brings it nearer to monotheism, is the dualistic idea that there are two opposing principles in the Universe, one good and the other evil, which are locked in perpetual conflict. This can be seen particularly in Persian Zoroasterianism, but echoes of it are to be found in the God-v.-Satan idea in traditional Christianity.

(c) *Henotheistic Systems*. These are related to polytheism except that in henotheistic systems, worship of one god or set of gods is regarded as paramount even though the 'reality' of other gods is recognized. Jahwism in Ancient Israel would be a good example of this. Many of the Old Testament prophets although enjoining loyalty to Jahweh only, accepted the presence of other gods while regarding them as inferior.

(d) *Pantheistic Systems*. These are where there is, strictly speaking, no deity, at least not in any personalized sense. Pantheism literally means 'all is God'; God is thus equated with all things, as in traditional Buddhism, or with the principle governing all things, as in ancient Taoism.

There are other systems which occupy a kind of indeterminate category, Confucianism would be a case in point. This is really an ethical philosophy which in its ancient form in China encouraged worship of the traditional gods and reverence for the ancestors. It is doubtful whether it qualifies as a religion at all. This necessarily involves the much-vexed question of how religion should be defined anyway—a problem that is still not satisfactorily resolved.

(ii) *Revealed Religions Frequently Develop a Written Tradition*
After an initial period of oral tradition, when the revelation or 'message' is simply transmitted by word of mouth, the tradition is usually committed to writing. These 'scriptures' are familiar features of high religions; the Muslim Koran, the Hindu Vedas and of course the 'Biblia', the collections of books of the Jewish and Christian traditions.

Scriptures are written for a number of reasons. Most commonly they act as aids to the rituals of their respective movements; they are the means whereby the traditions are preserved and communicated to subsequent generations. They can also be used to refute criticisms of the movements. In the Christian tradition, parts of the New Testament were undoubtedly written for this purpose; these 'apologias' constituted reasoned defences of the faith against the hostile attacks of critics and heterodox adherents who threatened to undermine the uncertain unity of the new movement.

Scriptures represent the crystallization of the early thinking of a movement. The message becomes 'set', as it were, for all time. What may have begun as a codification of the tradition for convert instruction, becomes a means of perpetuating 'everlasting' truths. Historically, this has given rise in many movements to the necessity of literate priesthoods which have acted—and still act to a lesser extent—as guardians and interpreters of the scriptures. Inevitably, these functions have served to enhance their status and increase their authority.

(iii) *Revealed Religions can be Dogmatic and Militant*

At certain phases of their development, religious movements may exhibit a surprising flexibility. Under certain circumstances, it pays to be adaptable. Although what makes a particular faith passive or militant may not be determined solely by external conditions. The internal ethic of certain movements is also very important. For example, Christianity has produced certain forms of Catholicism and Presbyterianism which have been extremely militant; it has also produced the Quakers who are not. And to complicate matters still further, the same tradition has also given rise to the Jehovah's Witnesses who are very dogmatic but so non-militant that they have been frequently persecuted for their pacifism.

Of course, the term militant can be used to mean aggressively evangelistic, but more accurately it is used to denote the willingness to advance the interests of a movement by military means. This policy has been extensively adopted by certain forms of Christianity and by Islam, on the other hand it has never been a general practice of Buddhism.

This militancy exhibited by some religions, although ostensibly for 'spiritual' purposes, may have a largely political function. Movements which try to establish earthly theocracies rarely act out of pure motives. Governmental authority which is established in the name of God has to be exercised arbitrarily by men. We have already seen that no form of control is more efficient and inexpensive than control exercised through belief.

Alternatively, militancy may be justified on the basis that men must be converted 'for the good of their souls'. This meant, under the medieval Inquisition, that the body might be tortured and subsequently destroyed in the interests of the soul. Immortal concerns outweighed temporal discomforts. It does not seem seriously to have occurred to anyone concerned that these interests were not necessarily incompatible.

(iv) *Revealed Religions are Usually Expansionist and Universalistic*

This follows logically from the previous point. Revealed religions have a 'message' which must be proclaimed. There is a 'truth' which everyone must share. Admittedly, in some religions, there has been some variety of interpretation and consequently some division of intention in this matter. Islam was divided on this issue in its early days, and Judaism has probably never been a universalistic religion in the full sense of the term. This same problem vitiated early Christianity, where the 'Jerusalem school' under James obviously wanted to confine Christianity to Jewish converts, whereas Paul argued for Gentile inclusion. This universalistic emphasis was already quite explicit in certain aspects of Jesus' teaching, particularly in certain parables, viz. the Labourers in the Vineyard (Matthew 19) and the much misinterpreted Prodigal Son (Luke 15).

High or world religions have sometimes had early phases when they restricted their membership to certain groups, and the faith was confined to a privileged minority. But such movements are, by definition, 'open' and are therefore prepared to admit into membership people of any previous persuasion, though few actively proselytize to this end. Christianity is the main exception in this, although other faiths, particularly Buddhism, have had proselytizing periods in their histories.

(v) *Revealed Religions Normally have Well-developed Cosmologies*
A cosmology is an explanatory system which offers a reasonably comprehensive set of answers to the problems relating to man's place in the universe. The explanations are of a mythico-spiritual kind and do not permit of either scientific validation or refutation.

In various ways, religions try to cope with what is technically known as the problem of theodicy, i.e. the attempt to explain the ways of God or the gods to man. The problems of evil, of suffering and death, all come within this category. One way of meeting these difficulties is in the provision of an insistent eschatology, i.e. in a clear doctrine of the 'last things'. This may take the form of a fulfilment in this world which holds that the kingdom of God or gods, will be set up on earth. Or it may take an other-worldly fulfilment form which maintains that punishments and rewards will be meted out after death in some future existence. Both these views can be found in different Christian groups.

(vi) *Revealed Religions Rehearse their Doctrines in Ritual*
Of course, ritual is a feature of all religious systems, but in high religions it takes particularly highly developed forms. Sometimes the beliefs are celebrated in special festivals and, more significantly, in cultic practices. Singular ritual acts often dramatize the essential doctrines of the system.

The Mass of the Roman Catholics involves a 're-enactment' of central Christian beliefs, and adult baptism practised by Baptists and others, constitutes a dramatic identity-mime. It may be that the psychological impact of participation in these ceremonies is more important to those concerned than the actual details of theology which underlie them. In practice, they are probably inextricably linked in the mind of the believer, although the act is experienced whilst the theology may not be clearly understood. To him, the very process of participation may be the most effective way of sharing the founding Revelation.

SOME RESERVATIONS ABOUT REVELATION

The problem of deciding what are the necessary criteria for assessing trustworthy revelations has never been satisfactorily resolved [4]. The two connected forms of the problem can be simply stated like this: if God/gods give revelations to men:

(a) How can we know in any given instance whether or not it is a 'true' revelation?
(b) If we think it is, how can we know that we understand it correctly?

Perhaps a brief outline of the kind of answers that have been given will help us to find our own answers for these questions.

(i) *The Subjective Certainty Answer*

This simply consists of insisting that one can know inwardly or intuitively. Some people argue that they 'just know' something to be true even though it cannot be verified empirically. The difficulty with this kind of inward 'knowledge' is that it can be, and has been, used to justify every variety of religious fanaticism. The worst excesses of religious persecution have followed from objective 'certainty'. We have already noted many instances of this in several religious systems.

The problem still remains: how is one to *know* that the revelation is 'real'? Even the most devout believers have been in doubt as to the source of their revelations. Christian mystics have maintained that the Evil One sometimes poses as 'an angel of light', and Martin Luther was so sure of alternative agencies that he even claimed to have thrown an inkpot at the Devil on one occasion!

It is obvious that the subjective certainty answer may be sufficient for the subject, but it does not always persuade other people.

(ii) *The 'By-Their-Fruits-Ye-Shall-Know-Them' Answer*
Some claim that this is the only real 'proof'. The results of a purported revelation are held to demonstrate its authenticity. These show whether it is true or false, good or evil.

But here again, the problem still exists—but at one remove. The 'fruits' answer presupposes that we always know what is good or evil, or at least what actions are likely to serve the interests of good and evil. If we think we know, how can we be certain that a particular course of action will have the correct results? For example, if, as most would agree, nuclear war is evil, is it 'right' to manufacture nuclear weapons as a possible deterrent? The Christian clergy are divided on this matter because in this case the issue is not clear. It may simply be a question of choosing the lesser of two evils—whichever that is. And this is only one of many issues of this kind.

There is yet another problem relating to the 'fruits' argument. Are we thinking of the 'fruits' in the recipient of the revelation, or the 'fruits' in terms of their wider historical effects? Recipients were often personally devout men, but either directly or indirectly their effects upon history were sometimes little short of disastrous. One thinks of, say, the dedicated thirteenth-century Saint Dominic whose teaching lay behind the medieval Inquisition which resulted in the murder of thousands. It can hardly be contested that the 'by-their-fruits' answer begs too many questions.

(iii) *The If-Its-In-Accordance-With-Tradition Answer*
This was considered before when we asked if people really had religious experiences. It has been maintained that revelations are genuine if they are in line with the traditions of the system. This argument obviously has its own kind of logic. *If* the tradition is 'true', it follows that all further revelations must conform to that tradition in order to qualify as 'genuine'. If they do not, it is argued that they must be *ipso facto* spurious.

Needless to say, this kind of answer makes two rather sweeping assumptions, namely, that the original tradition is true, and that the guardians of that tradition—who will almost certainly be priests or holy men of some kind—know how to judge all additional revelations. So, for instance, the Roman Church can accept the revelations of Saint Francis of Assisi, doubt the authenticity of Joan of Arc's 'voices' for five hundred years (she became Saint Joan only in 1920), and completely reject the reforming 'truths' of Luther and Calvin. And all this is not to mention the difficulties that science has had in its ongoing controversy with the Church. It can be argued that most of these derived from the stubborn insistence of the churchmen that they alone knew what could and what could not be reconciled with the original tradition.

(iv) *The Revelation-Must-Be-Reasonable Answer*

This speaks for itself. Here the assumption is that someone—again presumably those who administer the system—knows what is reasonable. How can one judge? Experience shows that what is considered to be reasonable varies with the occasion and with the tradition. Indeed, there may well be arguments about this within the *same* tradition. For example, the notion that the genuineness of the New Testament revelation can be judged on the basis of its miraculous content is still in dispute. Some insist that on rational grounds the miraculous should be dismissed entirely. Others, would distinguish, again on rational or 'common-sense' grounds, between the more 'reasonable' miracles such as those concerned with healing, and the seemingly 'unreasonable' miracles of, say the coin in the fish's mouth (Matthew 17: 24–7) and the wine-making at the marriage-feast at Cana (John 2: 1–11).

Implicit also in the reasonable revelations argument is the assumption that revelations must be reasonable if they are to appeal to reasonable men. The objections to this should be obvious. History has certainly not proved that reason has been indissolubly linked with human kind. To suggest that men are always or even primarily motivated by rational considerations is probably to make the biggest assumption of all.

(v) *The Revelation-Should-Not-Be-Wholly-Explicable-In-Naturalistic-Terms Answer*

This, of course, conflicts with the previous argument. Here the assumption is that a revelation which can be explained is hardly worth having. It is really a corollary of the view that a god who can be explained is not really a god; the truly supernatural cannot be reduced to naturalistic propositions. Revelations must be perplexing to be satisfying.

There is undoubtedly a certain logic in this idea also, but its weakness lies in the fact that the general form of the argument could apply to all manner of inexplicable phenomena which can hardly be classified as revelations. It could, for instance, cover various kinds of psychic phenomena; apparitions, poltergeists and the like which would not normally be thought of as the media of supernatural communications.

In a rather more specific sense, the notion that revelations should not be wholly explicable in naturalistic terms brings us back to the idea of the miraculous as a validation of the supernatural. Do the gods manifest themselves in the baffling and the uncanny? Is the 'unnatural' a sure sign of their presence? One of the main difficulties with this line of approach is that miracles are usually only accepted as 'proofs' by those who are predisposed to accept them in the first place. Those who are not, are rarely convinced. Again there is a conflict in the traditions. Many Jews will not accept the stories of New Testament miracles, and many Christians are not keen on some Old Testament miracles, and neither are particularly smitten by some of the wonders recounted by Muslims. And so it goes on.

When this is applied more generally to the idea of revelation, similar problems arise. In Spiritualist practices, for example, the message of the medium is only likely to be accepted by those who are prepared to make certain *a priori* assumptions, namely that there is another dimension from whence the 'messages' come, that such messages can be communicated, and that this communication can take place in this particular way. Acceptance of revelation pre-supposes a *will to believe* and a coming to terms with intellectual doubts.

REVELATION AS A LOGICAL POSSIBILITY

Certain phenomena of history and experience which cannot easily be explained within a scientific framework can only point to the *possibility* of revelation. They do not, in themselves, represent substantiating instances of supernatural communication. Should these, therefore, be entirely discounted, or should they be regarded more 'openly'?

How to distinguish between revelation traditions remains an apparently insuperable problem. The 'fruits-of-revelation' solution taken together with the argument that revelations should be 'reasonable', can only be partial answers. It is patently ridiculous to accept every claimed revelation as 'true', but to insist that they are therefore equally untrue, may be to throw a very persistent baby out with the bathwater. Perhaps we could, therefore, try to reassess the situation by taking a number of logically connected steps:

(i) An unbiased scientific approach must be prepared to admit the possibility of a dimension of reality outside our own. This may savour of wishful thinking or science fiction, but then it is a truism to state that the science fiction of yesterday is the actuality of today.

Let's take a fairly simple analogy. A person observes an ant in the garden; if he is a trained entymologist, he may be able to describe the ant's characteristics and even predict its patterns of behaviour. The ant and its observer share the same world, the same town, the same garden, yet the ant will only be dimly aware—if indeed it is aware at all—of an order of reality outside its own circumscribed ant-conscious world. If this is true of the ant, could it also be true of humans? Are we so 'advanced' as to dismiss this out of hand as an impossibility? Could there not conceivably be an order of reality which we, the observed, only vaguely perceive, and which sometimes intrudes upon our consciousness? [5]

(ii) If such an order exists, can we, therefore, admit a second possibility, namely, that what we call the universe is invested with some purpose? Biologists are divided as to whether to admit the possibility of purpose as a legitimate scientific category. Once it is conceded that organisms may have purpose, as distinct from mere functions—although even this idea has purposive overtones—the speculations are unbounded. The problem is that purpose suggests someone who purposes, in the same way that the notion of creation suggests a creator. Scientifically this is an unverifiable yet rather disturbing idea.

(iii) Given these assumptions, there follows a third possibility. If there *is* an other-dimensional purposive mind of which the 'universe' including mankind is a physical expression, does it not seem logical that these purposes might be made explicit in what we term history and experience? This admits the possibility of revelation, but it also poses the problem of why such revelations are not unambiguous. But this, in turn, can be partly countered by the argument that any communication must be made in ways which do not violate the exercise of human volition. In other words, revelations should be calculated to inspire trust, not generate fear. This is the kind of argument which can be used both to explain and to justify the God-in-human-form type of revelation such as that which underlies Christianity.

The problem is really so involved that it is tempting to dismiss the whole idea. Some revelation claims are very far-fetched, and many are positively bizarre. But there are other alternatives.

Logically, one does not have to refute a universally negative statement such as 'all revelations are false' by the universally positive statement, 'all revelations are true'. Only one 'true' revelation is needed to counter the negative contention. Put a little more technically, a particular positive will always refute a universal negative. To give a simple yet topical example, the insistence that all Unidentified Flying Object stories are false only needs one true instance to prove the case.

Men have wondered for generations if there is life 'out there', and if only *one un*explained sighting is correct—despite all those hundreds of sightings which have been otherwise explained—the case is *proven*.

Its rather similar with revelations. If only one genuine case could be proved, the thing that men have questioned since the dawn of history would be resolved; there is another reality apart from our own.

For those who cannot make these necessary assumptions, the 'leap of faith' is difficult. Intellectual arguments can never be entirely convincing. Unsatisfactory as some may feel it to be, faith is still an indispensable prerequisite to an acceptance of the supernatural.

9 The Earth seen from the Moon

References

Chapter One

1 Karl Popper, *The Poverty of Historicism*, Routledge, 1960.
2 H. Schilling, *Science and Religion*. Allen & Unwin.
3 As per Sigmund Freud. See C. E. M. Joad, *Guide to Modern Thought*, Faber, 1948.

Chapter Two

1 J. M. Yinger, *Sociology Looks at Religion*, Collier-Macmillan, 1963, pp. 50–6.
2 Wilson Wallis, *Messiahs, Their Role in Civilisation*, Washington, 1943.
3 Quoted by Allan Eister, *Drawing Room Conversion*, Duke University Press, 1950, p. 126.
4 Ibid., p. 140.
5 Ibid., p. 144.
6 E.g. see Emile Durkheim, *Elementary Forms of the Religious Life* (1915), Allen & Unwin, 1968.
7 F. M. Davenport, *Primitive Traits in Religious Revivals*, Macmillan, 1906.
8 See Michael Argyle, *Religious Behaviour*, Routledge, 1958, p. 54.
9 See J. Leuba, *The Psychology of Religious Mysticism*, Kegan Paul, 1925.
10 Weston La Barre, *The Peyote Cult*, Yale University, 1938.
11 Argyle, op. cit., p. 171.

Chapter Three

1 Eric Waterhouse, *The Dawn of Religion*, p. 24.
2 Herbert Spencer, *Principles of Sociology* (1876–1896), Macmillan, 1969.
3 Edward Tylor, *Primitive Culture* (1872),
4 W. Robertson Smith, *Religion of the Semites* (1880)
5 Sigmund Freud, *Totem and Taboo* (1918), Routledge, 1950.
6 Emile Durkheim, *Elementary Forms of the Religious Life* (1915), Allen & Unwin, 1968.
7 N.B. The Biblical story in the Book of Genesis of Cain and Abel. This may represent—in the form of a myth—the conflict which might have occurred between the Pastoralists (Abel, 'the keeper of sheep') and the Cultivators (Cain, 'the tiller of the ground'), at a very early period.
8 Raymond Firth, *Human Types* (1958), Sphere, 1970.

Chapter Four

1 Compare, for example, Royston Pike, *Encyclopaedia of Religion*, Allen & Unwin, 1951; and Horton Davies, *Christian Deviations*, S.C.M., 1954.
2 E. Isichei, 'English Quakers' in Bryan Wilson (ed.), *Patterns of Sectarianism*, Heinemann, 1967.
3 T. Clarkson, *A Portrait of Quakerism*, London, 1807.
4 See particularly Alan Moorehead, *The White Nile*, H. Hamilton, 1971; *The Blue Nile*, H. Hamilton, 1962; *The Fatal Impact*, H. Hamilton, 1966.
5 Of whom perhaps 12 million died in transit. Frank Tannenbaum, *Slave and Citizen*, 1948.
6 See E. Kellett, *A Short History of Religions*, Pelican, 1962.

Chapter Five

1 E. K. Nottingham, *Religion—a Sociological View*, Random House, 1971, p. 2.
2 Job 28: 12–13 (R.S.V.).
3 E. Gellner, 'Is Belief Really Necessary?', Hibbert Journal, October 1957.
4 E. Durkheim, *Elementary Forms of the Religious Life* (1915), Allen & Unwin, 1968, p. 431.
5 See A. R. Radcliffe-Brown, *Structure and Function in Primitive Society*, Cohen & West, 1952.
6 Luke 18: 29–30 (R.S.V.).
7 Thornton Wilder, *Heaven's My Destination*, Longman, 1968.
8 See Bryan Wilson, *Sects and Society*, Heinemann, 1961.
9 J. Rex and R. Moore, *Race, Community and Conflict*, O.U.P., 1969.
10 See Michael Argyle, *Religious Behaviour*, Routledge, 1958, pp. 147 51.
11 This is a notoriously difficult problem. Those most conscious of status deprivation need not necessarily be of the working classes. Also, so much depends on how to define 'religious'; sociologists are often content to do this statistically, i.e. in terms of church attendance figures. (See Volume 1, Chapter Six.)
12 I Thessalonians 5: 2.
13 See Peter Worsley, *The Trumpet Shall Sound*, Paladin, 1970.
14 See C. S. Lewis, *Miracles*, Fontana, 1960; *Mere Christianity*, Fontana, 1970.
15 Will Herberg, *Protestant, Catholic, Jew*, Doubleday, 1955.
16 N.B. That in the USA affiliation figures are exceeded by attendance ratings; this is the opposite of the situation in the UK.
17 See J. Milton Yinger, *Sociology Looks at Religion*, Macmillan, 1963.
18 See David Martin, *Pacifism*, Routledge, 1967.

Chapter Six

1 S. F. Nadel, *Witchcraft in Four African Societies*.
2 Philip Mayer, 'Witches' in Max Marwick (ed.), *Witchcraft and Sorcery*, Penguin, 1971.
3 I.e. by the anthropologist. E. E. Evans-Pritchard, *Witchcraft, Oracles and Magic among the Azande*, O.U.P., 1951.
4 See J. and E. Krige, 'The Lovedu of the Transvaal' in D. Forde (ed.), *African Worlds*, O.U.P., 1963.
5 See Georges Roux, *Ancient Iraq*, Allen & Unwin, 1964.
6 Sir Leonard Woolley, *Ur of the Chaldees*, Penguin, 1938.
7 For example, see Bryan Wilson, *Religion in a Secular Society*, Watts, 1966.
8 For example, G. Nelson and R. Clews, *Mobility and Religious Commitment*, University of Birmingham, 1971.
9 Wilson, op. cit., p. 14.
10 Note especially. W. Herberg, *Protestant, Catholic, Jew*, Doubleday, 1955; and P. Berger, *The Noise of Solemn Assemblies*, Doubleday, 1961.

Chapter Seven

1 See Arthur Koestler, *The Lotus and the Robot*, Hutchinson, 1966.
2 For example, J. Wach, *The Sociology of Religion*, University Chicago Press, 1944.
3 Max Weber, *The Sociology of Religion*, Methuen, 1965.
4 See W. Kaufmann, *Critique of Religion and Philosophy*, Faber, 1959.
5 See also Peter Berger, *A Rumour of Angels*, Penguin 1970.

Index

Aborigines (Arunta) 54
Allegories 22–3
Amos—*see* Prophets
Anabaptists 94
Ancestor cults 51–3, 55–7
Animism 53–4, 55–7
Anthropology 51–2, 99
Archaeology 51–2
Aristotle 13
Artemis 61
Ashurnasirpal II—*see* Assyria
Asiatic tribes 34–5
Assyria (Assyrian) 106, 108–9
Athens 105
Azande 100–2
Aztecs 45, 104

Babylonia, ancient 50, 62—*see also* Sumeria
Baptists 73–4, 123
Bernadette of Lourdes 117
Bible—*see* Scriptures, Old Testament, New Testament
Bigamists 81
Black Muslims 94
Buchman, Frank 39
Buddha (Buddhism) 65, 73, 94
Bunyan, J., *Pilgrim's Progress* 23

Calvin, J. 126
China, classical 52, 57, 76, 120
Charisma 116–19
Christening 24
Christianity as a system 23, 38, 65, 69, 71*ff*, 83–4, 119*ff*
  beliefs and practices 24–5, 65, 73*ff*, 91, 113, 115*ff*
  and the State 25–6
Colonialism 78–9
Concepts 24
Confucius (Confucianism) 75–6, 120
Cosmologies, world-views 123
Creation 27–8
Crusades 80, 83–4
Cults: snake-handling 42
  voodoo 42

Delphic oracle 105
Diffusion, and religious ideas 50–1
Dominic, Saint 94, 125
Drugs, and religion 44–7, 53
Dualism 120
Durkheim, Emile 54–5

Egypt, ancient 49–50, 53, 65
Einstein, Albert 27
Elijah, and the prophets of Baal 42
Elisha 65
Ethnocentricity 57
Evangelicalism 70, 77–81
Evil, problem of 123

Fascism 19
Francis, Saint 94, 126
Freud, Sigmund 47, 54–5

Gandhi 118
Gautama—*see* Buddha
Gifts of the Spirit—*see* Pentecostals
Graham, Billy 43–4
Greece, ancient 51–2, 57, 104–7
Gurus 36, 38

Har-maggedon 70
Headhunting (Sarawak) 78
Hebrews 37, 120
Hesiod 104
Henotheistic systems 120
Hinduism 36, 49, 62–3, 73, 94, 120–1
Hitler—*see* Nazis
Hittites 50
Homer 104
Homosexuals 81

Inquisition, especially the Spanish Inquisition 80–1, 122, 125
Iroquois 37
Islam (Muslims) 38, 63, 73, 77*ff*, 83–4, 94, 119, 120–1, 127
Israel (Israelites)—*see* Hebrews

James, the Apostle 122
Jehovah (Jahweh; Yahweh) 64, 70, 120
Jehovah's Witnesses 69–70, 119, 121
Jesus of Nazareth 23, 27, 38–9, 64, 70, 71, 117–18, 122
Jews, and Jewish tribes 80–1, 127
Joan of Arc 20, 34, 117, 126
Job, Book of 85
Judaism 38, 73, 77*ff*, 93, 119, 121
Judgements:
  aesthetic 19
  moral 19
  scientific 20–1

Kikuyu 86
Korongo 100
Krishna—*see* Hinduism

Leo X, Pope 94
Livingstone, David 79
Lourdes 34
Lovedu 102–4
LSD—*see* Drugs
Lugbara 51–2
Luther, Martin 94, 114, 118, 124, 126

Mahdi 94
Marriage forms 49–50
Marx (Marxists) 94, 111–12
Medieval society 91, 106
Melanesia 54, 89–90, 97
Mescaline—*see* Drugs
Mesakin 100
Messiah (messianism) 38–9, 71
Mexican tribes 45–6
Methodists (Methodism) 78, 118
Millennialism 89
Militancy and religion 77–81, 94, 121–2
Miracles 29–30, 34–5, 126–7
Missionary movements—*see* Evangelicalism
Monotheistic systems 119
Monarchy 25–6
Moral Rearmament (Oxford Group Movement) 39–40
Mormons 118
Moses 115
Muhammed—*see* Islam
Myths 22–3

Navaho Indians 100
Nazis (Nazism) 44, 57, 70, 117–18
New Testament 23, 25, 27, 35, 41, 61, 68, 78, 88, 121–2, 126
Nineveh—*see* Assyria
Nonconformity 24, 88
Nuclear weapons 125

Old Testament 22, 42, 62, 64–5, 85, 120
Ontological arguments 90

Pacifism 71
Paleolithic cultures 59
Pantheistic systems 120
Paul, the Apostle 35, 41, 78–9, 89, 115–16, 122
Pentecostals (Pentecostalism) 40–1, 89, 110–11
Peter the Hermit 83
Plato 90
Polynesia 63–4, 86
Polytheistic systems 119–20
Prayer and rationality 110–11
Presbyterianism 121
Primitive societies:
categories 58–9
Procustes (procrusteanism) 55
Prophets (prophecy) 36–8, 42, 133, 120
Psychic phenomena 127–8
Psychology, and psychological explanations 46–7

Quakers (Society of Friends) 70, 74–5, 121

Reformation 94, 114
Religion and revolution 93–5
Religion in USA 91–2, 110
Religious education 12
Religious experiences 33*ff*, 53, 113*ff*
Religious explanations 86*ff*, 98*ff*, 115*ff*, 124*ff*
Religious ideologies 12
Religious 'proofs' 27–31
Religious symbolism 23–4, 99
Religious systems (classification) 67*ff*
Religious 'truth' 17*ff*, 120*ff*
Revelation 113*ff*
Revivalism 44—*see also* Evangelicalism
Richard I (Lionheart) 83
Rituals:
fertility 59–63
hunting 59
intercourse and sacred prostitution 62
and fear 63–4
and values 99, 123
Rome, ancient 24–5, 51–2, 83–4
Roman Catholicism 34, 46, 61, 80–1, 93–4, 109, 114, 121, 123, 126
Russell, A. J. 39–40

Sacrifice 56, 58, 62, 64
Salvation Army 73–4
Saracens—*see* Crusades
Satan (Evil One) 70, 120, 124
Science and religion 20–2, 27–8, 85
Scriptures 28–9, 120–1
Secularisation 73, 92–3
Sex and religion 62, 71, 78
Shakers 70–2
Shamen 35
Shaw, G. B. 19
Shinto 65
Sikhism 36
Simon Stylites 118
Slaving 79
Smith, W. Robertson 54
Socialist philosophy 18–19
Sociology 'perspectives' 11–12
and religious 'verities' 13–14, 30–1
Socrates 105
'Speaking in Tongues 29, 40–1 —*see also* Pentecostals
Spencer, Herbert 52, 55
Spiritualists 29, 127–8
Stages of development 56–7

Sumeria 106–8
Suttee 78

Taboo 65, 86
Taoism 120
Theodicy, problem of 123
Tikopia 62
Timur (the Tartar) 118
Totemism 54–7
Trobriand Islands—*see* Melanesia
Tutankhamun 65

Unidentified Flying Objects
129–30
Unitarianism 75–6
Ur—*see* Sumeria

Vallabhis—*see* Hinduism
Virgin Mary 34, 61, 117

Waterhouse, Eric 51
Wesley, John 42–3, 118
West Indian sects 89
Whitfield, George 42–3
Witchcraft 86, 99–102
Working classes and religion 89

Yoga 45–6, 114

Zeus 104
Zoroasterianism 120
Zulu 59, 101